W9-DIL-027

HANS URS VON BALTHASAR

# THE THREEFOLD GARLAND

HANS URS VON BALTHASAR

# THE THREEFOLD GARLAND

## THE WORLD'S SALVATION IN MARY'S PRAYER

TRANSLATED BY
ERASMO LEIVA-MERIKAKIS

IGNATIUS PRESS    SAN FRANCISCO

Title of the German original
*Der Dreifache Kranz*
© 1978 Johannesverlag
Einsiedeln, Switzerland

Cover by Victoria Hoke

With ecclesiastical approval
© 1982 Ignatius Press, San Francisco
All rights reserved
ISBN 0-89870-015-9
Library of Congress Catalogue Number 81-83569
Printed in the United States of America

# CONTENTS

## Third Garland: THE CONSUMMATION

# PREFACE

To read most any work of Hans Urs von Balthasar is to plunge into a bright ocean where the most familiar truths and events of faith take on a freshness and a splendor usually hidden from our dull vision. The chief instance of this in the present volume is perhaps the astounding meditation on the mystery of the Lord's Finding in the Temple by Mary and Joseph. To many this could seem a relatively minor event in the Gospel narrative, and yet to von Balthasar it affords the opportunity of developing a whole theology of the ascetic life in a nutshell.

This theologian never "discusses" theology as one might some interesting topic, with that erudite chattiness so common to modern theologians and which so quickly wearies the reader. Rather, it is Father von Balthasar's particular mission in the Church as theologian to invite us to enter into his own untiring contemplation of the mysteries of faith. His is a theology that not only derives from prayer and leads back to prayer, but one whose natural element and very life-blood is prayer. He does not construct propositions and theses to provide us with a theological "method of approach"; rather, he teaches us to see what he sees and to love what he loves, and why. He never raises himself or his profession above the object of theology, for he knows only too well that it is this Object itself—God's being and his actions with man— that determines the attitude, the work and the mission of the theologian, who in the end is nothing but a believer striving for ever-greater understanding and clarity concerning the things the Church has already taught him to know and to love.

The little book we here offer is a classical demonstration of the fact that the profoundest truths need not always be expressed in a technical or esoteric terminology for them to retain all their depth. Far from that: it is the simplicity of the well-chosen image, the directness of a sudden intuition, the whisper of a sentiment too delicate for words, that often best preserve and convey the whole range of intended meaning. A certain genius is needed to compress great richness into great simplicity, and in my opinion this book, without diluting it, contains the essence of von Balthasar's weightier tomes; and this is so, I may add, not in spite of the fact that the style here is non-technical, at times poetic and always full of prayer, but precisely *because* of these qualities. For this reason I would recommend these thoroughly accessible pages as perhaps the best possible introduction to the overwhelming and sometimes difficult work of Father von Balthasar. The long philosophical excursus and slow-motion expositions required elsewhere in his work are often the measure of his titanic effort in trying to bring the mind of the world, the imbalances of a given cultural epoch and the exigencies of reason a bit closer to the warmth and the life emanating from the loving Heart of God. But at the center, at the *point vierge*, this Heart's mystery itself is utterly crystalline—invisible and unproblematic as the very air we breathe.

Surely one outstanding trait of von Balthasar's thought is what I would call its "concentric vision". By this I mean that he never treats a subject in isolation from all those other subjects which are naturally bound to it, but sees them as interacting concentric circles, distinct yet inseparable and springing from a common center. The unity of the Paschal Mystery is certainly the determining source of this vision (presence of the

9

cross at the crib, the Lord's glorification in his death out of love . . . ); and, in extending this principle of concentric unity to all the mysteries of faith, von Balthasar is not merely trying to be methodologically consistent or original, but is exhibiting his theological obedience to the actual manner God has chosen to redeem man, a manner reflecting the very interior nature of God himself.

And so we have before us both the circle representing the reality of Christ and the circle of Mary, by divine choice utterly inseparable from one another. "You are wider than the heavens", the Eastern liturgy sings to the Holy Virgin, "for within yourself you have confined the unconfinable God." The question as to which circle contains which is as old at least as the Council of Ephesus (431): the Creator by his nature contains his creature, Mary, who by grace comes to contain the Creator! This, the essential paradox of Christianity, receives a terser, more Latin formulation from St. Catherine of Siena, who in her *Dialogue on Divine Providence* exclaims to her Lord: "We are Your image and You are our image" (IV, 13). The traditional iconographic representation of this mystery of awesome exchange teaches the dogmatic truth most graphically. The icon known as "Our Lady of the Sign" ("sign" here referring to the prophecy of Isaiah to Achaz) shows Mary offering Christ to the world from a "mandorla" on her breast, that is, from a "window to heaven" consisting of concentric circles and out of which appears the Savior. The Virgin herself, in turn, is surrounded by a greater mandorla.[1] Our Lady becomes the *Theotokos*—the conceiver, the bearer, the nurturer of God—not by a law of nature or of logic nor by the design of men, but because of the humble omnipotence of the *Philanthropos Kyrios*, the divine Lover of Mankind who, says St. Irenaeus, can make himself subject to his creature because, in him, compassion and omnipotence coincide (*Adversus haereses* III, 24).

In this sense *The Threefold Garland* is a companion volume that completes *Heart of the World*, also by Father von Balthasar and an earlier publication of the Ignatius Press. If *Heart* is a book about the love of the Redeemer for fickle man, about the human and suffering face and Heart of God, then the *Garland* is about the human Mother who gave God his Heart and thus made God's suffering— and the redemption—possible. The uncreated Lord cannot have a mother; the redeeming Lord must. And, because there are not two lords but one

[1] For a thorough exposition of the theology of icons, including splendid plates, see Leonid Ouspensky and Vladimir Lossky, *The Meaning of Icons* (Boston, Boston Book and Art Shop, 1952), esp. pp. 78f.

Lord, Mary unexplainably becomes both the Mother of God and the Mother of all those redeemed by the incarnate God, who wills that man should receive from Mary the life he has deposited in her corporeally. But because this life is actually himself, no one can be found in Christ who is not also found in Mary.

It is quite characteristic of von Balthasar's theology that his book about Mary should approach the Mother of God exclusively in her relationship to the redemptive mysteries of her Son. Without ever becoming polemical, von Balthasar illuminates the mystery of Mary's divine motherhood in a manner that should dispel Protestant fears of alleged Catholic and Orthodox "Mariolatry". The book's subtitle ("the world's salvation in Mary's prayer") at once provides the basis for all true Mariology: the Church's and the individual Christian's prayer *to* Mary is a movement *towards* Mary, towards the place of holiness Mary already occupies. Thus, Marian prayer (whether this means prayer to Mary or in the manner of Mary) is but the practical means of entering into and participating in the reality which Our Lady already embodies—that of being the "handmaid of the Lord" even (and especially!) in her glorification. By her very nature, Mary is incapable of being an end in herself. Nevertheless, this rather re-enforces than diminishes her role in the economy of redemption. Already in the second century, at the very dawn of Christian theology, we find St. Irenaeus combatting the Gnostic tendency to spiritualize and rationalize the central mystery of the faith, the Incarnation, to the point of its evaporation. And the vigorous bishop of Lyons binds together all his other arguments concerning the hard reality of the Lord's humanity and its redemptive effects by declaring that, through her obedience and her resulting conception of the Son of God, the Virgin Mother became "the cause of salvation both for herself and for all of mankind" (ὑπακούσασα ἑαυτῇ τε καὶ τῇ πάσῃ ἀνθρωπότητι αἰτία ἐγένετο σωτηρίας: III, 2). Mary already *is* what we *may be*, and being the physical Mother of the God-Man she provides the indispensable chamber for the espousals of God and man. God does not erase the paths he has once traced, and thus he cannot will for us to become sanctified, which is to say divinized, other than in the place where he himself became human: in the humble shrine of the Virgin's obedient heart.

Most important of all is the fact that this theological understanding of Mary's role in the economy of redemption does not remain at the level of speculation, but unconditionally occurs in the context of prayer. Von Balthasar introduces us to the meaning of Mary by making us adopt from the outset the fundamental attitude of Mary: silent waiting, humble serving, ready praise. Her every heartbeat prays: 'Let him come and do in me!' Is this passivity, or activity of the intensest sort?

The fact that this is a book about the rosary is only indirectly alluded to in the original title.[2] For von Balthasar wants to write a book not so much about the rosary as such as about the mysteries of the rosary, the praying and living of those mysteries, which is the only thing the rosary ought to be about in the first place. Often a religious practice can break away from the living movement of faith that originated it, and it becomes hardened as a separate thing in itself. In this case the author short-circuits a devotion that has perhaps at times become a mechanical convention or, merely, a Catholic shibboleth, in order to revitalize it from within. But this is not to say that von Balthasar intends to spiritualize the prayer of the rosary to the point that the beads slip from our hands and we are left with a vacuous, if authentic, *idea* of the Christian mysteries. The rosary, both as a practice and as a concrete instrument of prayer

[2] The German *kranz*, 'garland', is part of the word for 'rosary', *rosenkranz*, which thus means 'rose garland'.

14

occupying space, does after all remain a powerful invitation to prayer, a symbol of the unity and completeness of the mysteries of faith, a quasi-sacramental reminder of the knot of things human and divine effected by Christ in Mary and, most elementally, it remains something to clutch silently in moments of anguish. Our author often insists on the necessity and meaning of the repetition of the Hail Mary, and our saying the prayer with our lips (and our fingers!) as well as with our hearts and minds insures that its effect will penetrate all layers of our being. And this is not a barely concealed magical ritual, but Christian existentialism and psychological realism of the most fundamental kind.

The chapter-headings of the book call for some explanation to the non-German reader. You will note that each heading is in fact the sentence that concludes the first half of the Hail Mary. But after the name of Jesus a short phrase has been added that resumes the mystery of the rosary in question. Repeating the phrase proper to each mystery midway through each Hail Mary of that mystery is a very effective way of aiding the contemplative gaze to center on the event before it. This is the standard way of praying the rosary in Germanic countries, even for public recitation. And notice, further, that in every instance the phrase is a relative clause that defines the redemptive character of Jesus in some particular way. Thus, the Christocentric nature of the prayer of Mary is safeguarded, since the wonder of the Mother is comprehensible and receives its full splendor only when steeped in the wonder of the Son. These little meditative *clausulae* became widespread in German-speaking countries in the late Middle Ages. They were first introduced at the Charterhouse of St. Alban's at Trier and are attributed to the piety of Dom Dominic Eloynus (1384–1460), a monk of that house, who coined a different phrase for each of the fifty Hail Marys in a cycle. Later on this usage was simplified to only one clause per mystery. The practice soon spread among German-speaking Carthusian houses, very numerous at this time, and from there to the laity.[3] It can come as no surprise that a practice intended to quicken and deepen Marian prayer should have originated among the sons of St. Bruno, who to-date look upon their cells as the extension, in the Church, of Our Lady's silent

[3] For the full history of the devotion, see Yves Gourdel, O. Cart., "Le culte de la Très Sainte Vierge dans l'Ordre des Chartreux," in: Hubert du Manoir, S.J., ed., *Maria: Études sur la Sainte Vierge*, v. 2 (Paris, Beauchesne, 1952), pp. 657–675.

house at Nazareth where, at her side, God first dwelt among men.

This translation is dedicated to Deal Hudson, who asked me about Mary.

ERASMO LEIVA-MERIKAKIS

University of San Francisco
Feast of the Assumption
August 15, 1981

*Ave Maria!*

*Christian prayer can attain to God only along the path that God himself has trod; otherwise it stumbles out of the world and into the void, falling prey to the temptation of taking this void to be God or of taking God to be nothingness itself. God is not a worldly object, but neither is he a supraworldly thing to be aimed at and conquered, after making adequate technical preparations, by a kind of spiritual trip to the moon. God is infinite freedom, which opens up to us only on its own initiative. He not only addresses his Word to us, but makes it live among us. Thus, the Word that comes from God is also the Word that returns to him. The path between God and us has been trod in both directions: "I am the Way, the Truth and the Life." "I have come into the world as its Light so that no one who believes in me will remain in the darkness" (Jn 14:6; 12:46).*

19

But how has this "Way" reached us? How has the "Light" penetrated to us? How has the "Word" lived among us? For this had to happen if we were ever to set out for God along a road practicable by men. Otherwise the Light would have only shone into the darkness and the darkness would not have grasped it. The Light would have come into its domains—for the world belongs to God—but its subjects would not have welcomed it. Someone had to receive the Word, so unconditionally that it staked out a space in a human being in order there itself to become man, as the Child of a Mother.

We ourselves are not this Mother, who opens herself up and offers herself to God without holding anything back: none of us speaks to God the unconditional Yes. This is why the perfect assent always precedes us unsurpassably. And yet, if God's Word is really to reach us, it is indispensable that it become the Way which we humans can tread. It could not have become man in a heart only half-open to God, for the child is essentially dependent on its mother. It is nourished from her corporeal-spiritual substance; it is reared by her to genuine and fruitful humanness. The Mother's precedence ahead of us—essential for the establishing of the road between God and us—does not imply her isolation, but rather the opening up of the possibility of us too becoming assenters, the possibility of the Word reaching us, too, and of us reaching God in the Word. "Blessed is the womb that bore You and the breasts that nursed You. Yes, truly blessed are they who hear God's Word

20

and keep it" (Lk 11:27f). "Whoever does the will of my heavenly Father is to me a brother, a sister and a mother" (Mk 3:35).

Mary's abiding pre-cession is the basis of our own suc-cession. The community which binds God to man in her when he becomes a Child of man is the foundation of a community which binds us all together as children of God, a community which we call God's Church. The mother is the enduring presupposition, the source, the full realization of the Church, to which we can belong, if we only will it, as people under way to the perfect assent that sinks deep roots into our whole existence. Thus, we the half-finished can and must say "Hail, Mary!" to her who is whole, to her who introduces us and rears us to her wholeness. But it is not by separating her from the Son that we do this; for she is but the Answer while he is the Word.

The happening that occurs between the Son and the Mother is the center of the event of salvation, which can never lose its relevance because God's gracious self-revelation is always occurring at the present moment: the river can never become distanced from its source. If a person wants to participate in it he must plunge into this wellspring, into its inexhaustible mystery: that God's Word has really opened itself to us, that it has really been received among us and has really dwelt among us, that it has not returned to God alone but together with us. We can see what this means from the relationship between this Child and this Mother. She totally puts

21

herself at the Word's disposition that it may become flesh from her—flesh from her flesh. But as this Child grows up and gives his divine flesh for the reconciliation of the world with God, as he offers it as a eucharistic nourishment to all who receive the Word in faith, he draws into his own flesh those who welcome him, first of all his Mother, archetype and source of the Church. Both of them, Christ and Mary-the-Church, are thus "one flesh", one "body" by virtue of a reciprocal event: first, Christ is the receiver of Mary's earthly flesh; then Mary-the-Church becomes a partaker of his heavenly flesh. Insofar as only the Mother puts her flesh at the disposal of the Word's incarnation, she is "blessed among women"; but this is but the first movement leading to the second, whereby "blessed is the fruit of her womb, Jesus", who has elicited his answer from the earthly flesh, the answer of Mary-the-Church, and steadily continues to elicit it in the Eucharist. And he elicits it from us, too, the members of the body, who according to the purity and fullness of our assent can also become her fruitful members, her very womb.

Thus we, too, on mandate from God, may greet Mary together with the Angel, and, with Elizabeth, continually call her blessed since "God is with her"; in this manner we will be praying our way into her answer to the divine Word, into her word of assent, which is now no longer directed at her but which, together with her, is directed at God. "Hail, Mary!" is a training and

22

an integration into the prayer of Mary-the-Church. The official liturgical prayer of the Church, too—whether openly or hiddenly, consciously or unconsciously—is always Marian prayer. Nevertheless, here below we will never attain to Mary's perfection; as a constitutive condition for the way which is Christ, she is not only exemplary but archetypal, and for this reason we may constantly beg for her intercession—"now and at the hour of our death", that is, at every moment of our life, during the whole of which we remain strivers, such as have never quite attained their goal, and also at that hour when we are definitively and forcibly pushed onto our way to God, in that bitter and blessed transition when, for better or for worse, "as if through fire", we will have to learn the perfect word of assent. It is toward this hour that we live; as believers it is for this hour that we are training; and if it was only through prayer that Mary trained to utter her own word of assent, then we are truly unable to accomplish our assent by our own power: we must remain in an attitude of grateful attention looking to her who has truly been able to assent. This is why it makes sense if, at the end of the greeting —"now and at the hour of our death, Amen"—we always begin again at once with "Hail, Mary!"

By praising Mary in this circular fashion we are doing three things: we recognize the precedence of her accomplishment; we let her show us the way of the Church's assent to God; and, at the same time, we walk *along this way, which is her way only because upon it she is treading the path of her Son. And this way itself is forever circular: "I have gone forth from the Father and have come into the world. Now I will again leave the world and return to the Father" (Jn 16:28); the Son does this only once and yet time and again, since along this circular path he takes with him Mary and the Church and ourselves. If the world had been nothing but un-Marian darkness, if he had returned to the Father without the world, then he would not have fulfilled his task. But all of this happened for the sake of man, "so that they too may be where I am and that they may see my glory, which You, just Father, have given to me" (Jn 17:24f).*

FIRST GARLAND

# THE SOURCE

*And blessed is the fruit of your womb*

## JESUS

*whom you, O Virgin,
conceived of the Holy Spirit*

WHAT HAPPENED in the hidden alcove of Nazareth is the beaming over the world of the universal, catholic Light. In the Old Testament the heavens often opened and God's Word and Spirit often came forth from them; but never had the Spirit overshadowed the womb of a virgin. Everything that had occurred earlier was an anticipation, a preparation; now we see the fulfillment.

The Son of the Father allows himself to be borne into a human womb, and so the heavens open in a new way and reveal a threefold life in God. Everything proceeds from the Father, who remains invisible in the background. It is not he who becomes man; rather, he sends his eternal Son. But the Son lets himself be disposed of. Therefore, it is the Holy Spirit who is active: he accomplishes the will of the Father and bears the Son to where this will can be fulfilled "on earth as it is in heaven". God's interior vitality is manifested in the Incarnation, and with radical clarity in the Angel's three statements: "The Lord [the Father] is with You"; "You will give birth to the Son of the Most High"; "the Holy Spirit will overshadow You."

Everything proceeds from the Father's salvific will—even within God, insofar as the Son and the Spirit proceed eternally from his unfathomable and fruitful goodness. Son and Spirit, however, are not subordinate servants but equal in essence with the Father, and as such they participate in the very origin of the Father's gracious plan for the world, in equal agreement with the Father's thought, which in the end can be nothing other than ever greater goodness. This goodness has already given itself eternally to the Son and to the common Spirit of both; and therefore it can express itself to the world only in a triune manner: through the consent, indeed the offering of himself, of the Son, to make this goodness of the Father known effectively—even unto death on the cross; through the consent and self-offering of the Spirit ready to be engaged wholly in the service of this prodigal love of the Father in the self-surrender of the Son.

Everything proceeds from the "free and gracious decision" of the Father, and we are reminded of this by the "Our Father" that always returns between the decades of the "Hail Marys". It is to the Father that the first of all blessings goes. "Blessed be the God and Father of our Lord Jesus Christ, who has blessed us in Christ with every spiritual blessing in the heavenly places, even as he chose us in him before the foundation of the world, that we should be holy and blameless before him. He destined us in love to be his sons through Jesus Christ, according to the purpose of his will, to the praise of his glorious grace which he freely bestowed on us in the Beloved" (Eph 1:3–6). This upsurge of the Father's primal goodness is named the "mystery" (Eph 1:9) insofar as in Jesus Christ it overflows richly on all of humanity, both Jews and Gentiles. Here also belongs the fact "that you have been sealed with the Holy Spirit" (Eph 1:13), an event which first took place when this Spirit overshadowed the Virgin. Mary's blessing by Elizabeth is intended to reach, through Mary, the Fruit of her womb, and through this Fruit the Bestower of the Fruit, the eternal Father who is blessed by Paul because the Father, by his gracious decision, has blessed the whole of his creation.

Now the Son, wanting to make the Father's primal goodness graspable to the world, does not for all that undertake any activity on his own initiative: such a move would have put him in the limelight and not the Father. At the beginning of all his work there is found obedience: the readiness to let himself be disposed of by the Father according to his total will. This is a letting go, an indifference that never chooses this as opposed to that. Already the way from the bosom of the eternal Father to the womb of the temporal Mother is a path of obedience, the most difficult and consequential of ways, but one which is trod on mission from the Father. "See, I come to do Your will" (Heb 10:7).

The one who bears and drives him is the Spirit, the Spirit of the Father who sends and of the Son who obeys, the Spirit, therefore, who in his bearing and driving is both active and obedient. All along the Son's path through the world the Spirit will keep the Father's will before the Son's eyes, and in this way the Spirit, in a manner proper to spirit, will participate in the Son's obedience. The Father's outpouring of goodness—and this is grace—and the grateful reception of this goodness and grace are communicated and kept one in the person of the Spirit.

But the Word is to become man; the whole event of salvation is not an affair interior to God. To become man means to become the child of a mother, who in receiving God's seed must utter her total human word of assent. By no means is man overpowered and done violence to by God: nothing can or may be done to him to the possible consequences of which he does not consent in advance, even though he does not know what these consequences might be. Not only at present, but even later on, man ought not to be in a position to raise any objections against God, claiming that God has "deceived" and "outsmarted" him, as Jeremiah accused his God of doing: "You have seduced me, Yahweh, and I let myself be seduced. You clutched and overpowered me" (Jer 20:7). Rather, the Mother will, in anticipation, adopt the attitude of her Child, and this not only for a time but as embodying it forever: to be a pure answer to whatever the Father disposes. The eternal Word which the Father speaks into the world of men is itself always an answer to him; this answer must now resound from the world, and, indeed, from two persons, the Mother and the Son, for there is no such thing as an isolated human being. One is human only *with* others; the only humanity is cohumanity. This is so even and precisely in this perfect solitude of the Mother before God, a solitude in which she, hidden from the whole world, must be open to God in an inimitable manner. It is in this solitude that the community between God and man is founded, in the form of the community between mother and child, between person and person.

The Incarnation of the Word is the work of God. The redemption of the world does not occur because man is ready to say yes to God. Nor does the woman already have the man's seed in herself just because she is prepared to receive it. Insofar as it connotes the renunciation of autonomous decisions, obedience is passivity; but insofar as it is the readiness to receive everything, obedience is supreme activity. This is why obedience can be just as divine as the Father who disposes, why the woman who receives can have the same dignity as the man, why Mary's word of assent can be a participation in the quality of the Son's consent. This quality can only be bestowed on her in advance by God, not as something alien to her but as the capability for deepest self-realization. For God is eternal freedom, and, in giving himself, he can only free the creature to highest freedom.

God frees the creature to be both things inseparably in its word of assent: a grown, responsible woman, and a perfect child before God and in God. Or in other words: to be the bride's ready womb and nothing but a maiden. It would never have occurred to Mary to see her assent to God as a part of God's own work: she works with God

32

only in the sense that she lets him work in her. For this reason both things are true: that she is consulted, and that God disposes of her in advance ("You *will* bear a Son"). Even in this she is formed in conformity with her Son, who, being God's "only-begotten Son", henceforth becomes "God's servant".

In this mutual conformation Mary is the archetype and first cell of the Church, and the conformation is not only spiritual but, because of the bodily mystery existing between Mother and Child, it is also carnal. Both are "one flesh", just as the Church, once she attains to her perfect shape, will be the "Body of Christ". She is this in full truth when she participates in Mary's disposition. The Church, therefore, is a continuous movement toward her own center, which is already full reality. The sinful Church must therefore implore: "Pray for us sinners, now. . . ." If the Church were to seek her identity in her sinfulness and distance from the center—in "self-criticism"—she would be detaching herself from her true essential reality. The Church cannot consider herself in herself, in isolation; she must look to her origin in Mary. And in the end this can only be believed because, by virtue of grace, Mary gives an assent which is wholly free of sin. In so doing, however, Mary does not believe in herself, but in the deed of

33

God: "For the Almighty has done great things for me," which means that the Virgin has conceived of the Holy Spirit.

The sinful Church—we ourselves—receives the Lord's Body eucharistically. But none of us receives him wholly, according to his intention of giving himself to us. This is why, behind each of our communions, there stands the *Ecclesia immaculata*, the spotless Church who completes our imperfect assent. Only the Church in us communicates perfectly in Christ's Body, and this is one more reason to be thankful to her and adhere to her Spirit.

## 2

*And blessed is the fruit of your womb*

## JESUS

*whom you, O Virgin, took to Elizabeth*

M ARY RISES "WITH HASTE" to go visit her
cousin. This sudden departure is a result of
her obedience to the word of the Angel, who had
thus instructed her: "See, Elizabeth, your kins-
woman, has also conceived a son in her old age,
and this is the sixth month for her who was
thought to be sterile." Mary goes to Elizabeth's
in order to make herself useful; and it is almost
a secondary result that, because of Mary's visit,
the opportunity arises for the cousins to recognize
each other's grace and interchange their joy. Mary's
first thought is that Elizabeth is bearing a child,
and in going to her Mary brings her own Son
along.

When giving her assent Mary was alone, since
at receiving one's decisive mission for life, every-

one must stand alone before God and say yes; only after this is one again inserted into community in a new way. Henceforth this is the community of those who have also had to say yes and have also received a mandate from God: such is the community of the Church. It can happen that I already knew the person to whom I am now joined, as a purely worldly acquaintance or friend; but now the narrow, private space of our relationship broadens to become a much larger dimension that at the same time implies a more intimate contact between our individual spheres (through our missions) and a deeper expropriation that carries us out to what is objective, anonymous, catholic. In common we look to what has been given to us in common, in the Holy Spirit of the mission who here permeates the whole scene.

It may be that Mary felt a slight anxiety at what might be awaiting her in this new encounter. For she is not coming alone, but with something within her to which she has fully and fundamentally consented without nevertheless knowing its full compass. She is a vessel, a monstrance of the Word and Will of God become flesh. And she does not know how this center within her, around which she now has her life, will grow to full stature. She knows she has been expropriated into God's whole objective history of salvation, and

36

that at the same time she has been placed on a pedestal, since the center of this salvation history is here living and growing within her own center, eventually to emerge from her. But this does not arouse any panic in her, for by her consent she has surrendered to the double mystery: as a maiden, to vanish from sight, but as the bearer of God's Word, to come into full prominence. In the Magnificat she unites both things: all generations will call her blessed, and they shall never cease to look up to her; but she herself looks only to him "who has come to the help of his servant Israel, remembering his mercy as he had promised our fathers, Abraham and all his children."

Thus, she bears what she lets herself be borne by. And it is, quite simply, in this attitude that her faith consists. The faith of every member of the Church must take its bearings by her faith, which carries within itself a content greater than it can understand: this is why Mary's faith willingly lets itself be borne along by what it contains.

But precisely this attitude of the Mother is nothing other than her integration into the attitude of her Child. Every child must begin by letting itself be borne. And this Child in particular, even when it is big, will never outgrow its childhood: even when he acts as an adult he will always let himself be borne and impelled by the will of the Father as manifested to him by the Spirit. Now he is under-going his first, physical training as he is carried about bodily. It is a training as in a novitiate, when a person is ordered around like a child. This is the first training in what every Christian must always be able to do: let himself willingly "be led where you do not want to go", as Jesus will say to Peter. The child in the womb does not know where it is being borne. Nor will Jesus know where he is being "driven" by the Holy Spirit (Mk 1:12): it may, for instance, be into the wilderness and temp-tation. This attitude of letting himself be borne and driven will be perfected in the Eucharist: here the Son will hand himself over to both the holy and the unholy spirit of the Church in order to stand at the disposal of men who are not ready to receive him as who he is, who are not ready to let themselves be determined by his grace, by his attitude of obedience. Now as a child, later on as a man, and finally as a host, the Son will let himself be borne about as a thing that one can dispose of—and this is he who bears the sin of the world and, therefore, the world itself.

Only one—the Father in heaven—sees all of this, sees where the triune decision to save has led. In Mary, the Son is already under way; already he begins to be driven about in the world, and no one, not even the Father, can call him back. The

Father has entrusted him to the responsibility of the Mother, and she will have to deliver him into the hands of men who will do things to him which were not intended by the goodness of God's will to salvation. . . . But the Father encompasses all things, even this recalcitrant element. The destiny of the world and of God himself has begun rolling, and no one can throw himself into its spokes.

But already they arrive at a first stop. Mary enters Zachary's house and greets Elizabeth, who is immediately filled with the Holy Spirit and exclaims: "You are blessed among women, and blessed is the fruit of your body! . . . Blessed are you who have believed!" In the Spirit she recognizes what is happening to her; in the Spirit she marvels at what is coming to her: "Why does it befall me that the Mother of my Lord is coming to me?" Every Christian who has a living faith will marvel his whole life long—in both the knowing and the unknowing of faith—that such a thing could have happened to him. In every prayer this sense of astonishment should be awakened anew whenever being a Christian threatens to become a matter of habit.

The Spirit also shows Elizabeth very palpably why she must marvel in this situation, and how it is that in this person whom she knows so well it is the "Mother of my Lord" who is coming to her.

She herself indicates it: "For behold, as soon as your greeting struck my ear the child leapt for joy in my womb." The truly beautiful thing here is that it is by her own fruit that she realizes how blessed Mary's Fruit is, and that it is Mary, and not herself, who is therefore blessed, because "she has believed what was told her by the Lord." The grace that is in her, and which over the course of six months could almost have become habitual, now moves vigorously within her as if to admonish her that now is the time for real astonishment. This grace is her child. It is not she but the child that is first touched by the new grace: he is thus established in his mission as precursor, and it is only by the child's mission and its joy that the mother's happiness and accord are aroused. What better thing could happen to her than that this her child—the next generation—should come to salvation? This is a mentality which could be seen as summarizing the whole Old Testament: to be blessed in one's children. But it is abrogated in the New Testament: here it is the Child Jesus who, in his Mother, has himself chosen his forerunner, and in so doing has brought the Old Testament to completion.

In the very skillful delimiting of the four missions (of Jesus and Mary, of John and Elizabeth) we must come to recognize the active presence of the Holy Spirit. The fact that Elizabeth prays the words of the Hail Mary "with a loud voice" is, as always in the Bible, the sign that God is speaking through her mouth. The whole scene is one single inspiration containing multiple articulations. God's Spirit falls down vertically on the horizontal relationships between persons. It is the Spirit that motivates these relations, giving them fullness, depth, resonance. And the relationship between the Old and the New Testament appears here in the highest possible condensation, inseparably intertwined: the fullness of meaning of the Old Testament (in John) is bestowed by the New Testament (Jesus): "He who comes after me is ahead of me because he was before me," the Baptist will say (Jn 1:15).

And the Evangelist himself was drawn into the art of this scene by the Spirit. No one can just simply write this; it is like the distillate of a long, prayerful meditation during which, rose by rose, a garland is slowly woven which in the end comes wholly to repose in itself.

## 3
*And blessed is the fruit of your womb*

# JESUS

*to whom you, O Virgin, gave birth*

THE LONG TIME OF ANXIETY—"will I alone be enough for such a child?"—has come to an end; the Child is there, first of all as the same miracle which occurs at every birth: from one being we suddenly have two, and Eve's astonished cry is repeated every time: "Through God I have received a child!" (Gen 4:1). When a mother is holding her child in her arms for the first time, she always gives thanks, for she is conscious that she has not brought it forth of her own bodily and spiritual power: the child is something given. And of course a word of thanks to her husband is in order; but even the husband is amazed: he is even less responsible for the total result than is the woman. Even animals bear their young, but these are not personalities that are more and presuppose more than just a life-principle which

43

continues to develop. From every new person there radiates something of God's uniqueness. God himself came into play in this encounter of the parents. The depths of generation and conception reach down all the way to the eternal life of God.

With the Child to whom Mary has given birth this divine depth lies open in a very different way. Mary knows that she owes this Child not to any husband but to God alone. Thus, she is thankful in a double sense: as a mother is thankful to her husband and as both parents are thankful to God. What else does this mean, however, but that her Child, as a person, has not only been created directly by God, but that he himself is of divine provenance? In this she knows that she has not been used as a mere instrument, but that her human word of assent has been taken seriously. She is not only the pipe from the well through which God's gift has flowed; she and God together are source.

This is why she comes to see her own responsibility in a new way. She will have to be a mother to her child, physically and spiritually, feeding him with her milk, educating him and introducing him to the world of men, but above all to the world of God. At birth he detached himself from her in order to tread his way back to the Father

44

through the world. The Mother will not retain her Son by her; rather, she will renounce him and introduce him to her renunciation. The time will come—very soon indeed, and then time and again—when the Son will have learned his lesson so well that he will, in turn, introduce his Mother to *his* renunciation, one going beyond all human measure: "Did you not know that I must be about these things? . . ." "Who are my brothers and who is my mother? . . ." "Woman, behold your son!" He shows her how far an unconditional consent from God can lead, how wholly beyond itself.

In the act of being born there already begins the act of dying; and just as people flee from death, so do mothers cling to their children so that they will not go away from them and draw closer to death. In all truth, already at the birth the mother has been expropriated; she can accompany her fleeing child a piece down the road for as long as the child needs her, but this must happen already in renunciation. Something similar holds for all our works, especially for those that are most spiritual, most personal, most un-selfserving and therefore most fruitful. Once they have been realized they no longer belong to us; they have been handed over to God's providence for him to administer them.

From the Mother's disposition grows the disposition of the Church. The Church is not an external assembly of people brought together by a common religious purpose, but rather a reality which exists before we do and to which we owe what we are, through God and by the grace of God. No one helps himself to the sacraments; they are bestowed on a person as graces. In a very real sense Baptism, by which one is "born from God" (Jn 1:13), is also a birth from the Church. According to the Church Fathers, God's Word, proclaimed in a living way, is, like the sacraments, drunk from the breasts of the Church. It is here that we are nourished like the Child Jesus at his Mother's breast. The Church is responsible for us before God; she is to rear us in her pure and holy Spirit and not in our own. And since our birth from the Church is not a carnal birth, the Church can indeed start us off on our way to God, but she cannot and ought not to abandon us at that point; for the more mature we become as Christians, the more responsibly do we grow into her community. We become "ecclesial souls", persons of the Church who, for their part, have to become fruitful in the Church. Looking back on Mary from this perspective we realize that she, too, accompanied her Son to the last—even into his death and abandonment—and that he, too, took her along to the very end: all the way to the glorification of her whole existence with his in heaven.

In the background of this scene of birth there also stands Joseph, who renounces his own fatherhood and assumes the role of foster father assigned to him. He provides a particularly impressive example of Christian obedience, which can be a very difficult one to accept, especially in the physical sphere. For one can be poor by having given everything away once and for all, but one can be chaste only by a daily renunciation of something which is inalienable to man. And the forces stemming from this renunciation pass over imperceptibly into the work of Jesus, into the chastity that is lived by him and demanded of him. Unlike Mary, however, Joseph was not asked whether or not he wanted to renounce. It is not even explained to him how his wife has become pregnant. Only when he decides to dismiss her does God deign to enlighten him. The husband must be humiliated, precisely as the Son of God is about to tread the path of all humiliation.

In the vicinity of the manger there are shepherds. To them the angel has recalled all of the promises to Israel, and he has proclaimed the fulfillment of these promises as already taking place. What they find is a very modest confirmation of the fact that God is saying the truth: "They found

Mary and Joseph and the Child, which was lying in the manger." They encounter these persons and that is to be enough for them, and that *is* enough for them. Now that the divine Son is a Son of Man, no one can any longer bypass one's fellow man in one's yearning for revelations. God's Word has referred the shepherds to this sign; they must have enough humility and clairvoyance in order to perceive, in this "sign" of the Child wrapped in swaddling clothes, what God himself has designated.

Even God the Father has to learn this. How different now the appearance of his Son, whom he has begotten from his bosom from all eternity and who has always answered him and reciprocated him, being "his almighty Word"! And now this nursling, who still cannot even stutter, is supposed to be this almighty Word. . . . Moreover it has not occurred by a descending process of alteration but as if by an infinite plunge from omnipotence to impotence. And this is only the beginning of an impotence which later on will continue to deepen in his not being welcomed by his own, in his concealment and disfigurement to the point of unrecognizability. Perhaps the triune plan looked rather different when it was first conceived in eternal life, where the meaning and goal of the whole may be surveyed with a single glance; perhaps it looked different from now, when this swaddled Child lies before the eyes of the Father in indistinguishable ordinariness, in this stall exposed to all the winds of human indifference and disdain. . . .

But God's Spirit mediates: he has measured the whole road from exaltedness to lowliness and he bears witness to the Father that the descent into unrecognizability corresponds precisely to the triune design.

The Son finally entered into this "schema which is man" (Phil 2:7); here he has let himself be shaped, grown and birthed in the same passive manner in which he let himself be implanted in the Virgin's womb by the Spirit, "born of woman", subject to the laws of nature, soon to be subjected also to the Jewish laws at his circumcision and his presentation in the temple. These laws will fetter him more tightly than the swaddling clothes that now bind him. How his eternal and divine consciousness entered into this near-unconsciousness proper to a child is a mystery which we will never penetrate. Nevertheless: This Child is the Son; he is not—in addition to being a child—something wholly different somewhere else. In the meantime, his "repose in the bosom of the Father, his orientation to the Father" (Jn 1:18) has taken on the form of warmly being nestled in the arms of his Mother. Her prayerful assent to God may be expanded infinitely, until it reaches the measure of the Father's own consent to all this Christmas lowliness. This is why the Child can entrust himself to the Mother in the same way that he had from all eternity entrusted himself to the Father.

## 4

*And blessed is the fruit of your womb*

JESUS

*whom you, O Virgin,
offered up in the temple*

T HE PRESENTATION OF THE CHILD in the temple
by his virginal Mother combines three different aspects. All three correspond to the customary
Jewish law to which every first-born male child
and every mother had to submit, and in all three
cases these ordinary ceremonies attain a unique
significance. These are the Boy's circumcision,
the Mother's legal purification and the redemption of the first-born.

At the circumcision the Child is incorporated
into the People of God and, at the same time,
receives his name. Since the name had been determined in advance by the Angel, the circumcision,
too, is indispensable. From ancient times it was
the drastic form of embodying and making the
covenant definitive in the individual: "My covenant

in your flesh shall be an everlasting covenant"
(Gen 17:13). Paul will put Baptism in the place of
this drastic sign. Baptism, however, will by no
means imply a "spiritualization" of God's incarnation, but rather an even deeper entering into and
partaking of it. Not only an external organ, but
all of physical man is now to be circumcised, and
thus pass over to be God's property. In the biblical
sense, Jesus allows the sign "to be done" to his
flesh; in him it is unique because he is the whole
embodied covenant in person. Likewise the name
"Jeshuah" ("God saves"), until now very common, becomes a proper name whose meaning is
concretized in the unique figure of this Child.

Then, a month after the birth, comes the time
for the Mother's purification: "The days of her
purification had arrived." Luke softens it by saying
"of *their* purification" (Lk 2:22), in the plural, but
only Mary can be meant. It was the mother who,
according to the law, was considered unclean and
was not allowed to touch anything or to show
herself in the temple (Lev 12). The purification is
effected by a burnt offering and a sin offering. The
woman could also appear without the child; but in
this case, in which the three events are united, the
whole Holy Family is together. The tension between the universal law and the particular case
is this time even more blatant. The child that

submitted to the ceremony of circumcision was thereby marked as a member of the People that was expecting God's salvation—the Messiah. Likewise, the mother was stamped as an ordinary married woman who avowed that she had conceived this child from her husband and had given birth to him in the usual manner. But it is probable that Joseph's initial suspicion had also been entertained by others living in their proximity: that she had become pregnant illegitimately. And we can suppose that even later, when the Child had been recognized by Joseph, Mary had to continue to live under this suspicion.

Thirdly, connected here with the ceremony of purification, we have that of the redemption of the first-born male: he belongs to God and must be bought back from him (Ex 13:2ff; Num 18:15ff). In strict justice, the first-born male should be sacrificed to God, as was always the case with oxen, sheep and goats (Num 18:17). Whatever belongs to God and has been received as a gift from him can—as in the case of Abraham—be demanded back by God. Or God can take it back himself, as was the case of the tenth plague in Egypt. When Israel's first-born males were spared at that time, the Levites were consecrated to God as a substitute for them (Num 3:12f). The fact that God bestows all fertility is forever recalled by the prescription of the sacrifice of exchange, which only the father of a family could fulfill, not necessarily in Jerusalem but also by going to any priest in the country.

These three elements are brought together by the Evangelist even as he maintains the temporal distance between the circumcision and the purification. The meaning of all three symbolic actions is the sacrificial returning to God of what belongs to him, and this occurs in obedience with respect to the "law of Moses" or "of the Lord", as Luke repeats five times with incisive urgency. Not even the poor man is dispensed from this; thus, in place of a more expensive animal, Joseph brings the poor man's sacrifice of two doves. The Son became man under the sign of obedience, and no worldly necessity had required this of him; and also under the sign of obedience he enters the People of God, something which can only create a misunderstanding when seen from the outside. And into this his obedience he also draws along his Mother and his foster father. The first blood now flows—to no one's guilt: this is but the earnest money for the blood of the Passion, through which the true and only "purification" and "redemption" will be realized. Everything which had been image, symbol, ceremony is now surpassed interiorly by the reality, the lived reality which is what the many sacrifices always intended. But this occurs precisely within a deepened concealment —reaching to misunderstanding and scandal— whereby a free obedience submits to the prescriptions of the law. It is at just this that the mystery of the "presentation" aims: the Child is "sacrificed" ceremonially by his parents (as the Church would later sacrifice her Lord at Holy Mass) and the Child "sacrifices" his Mother and his family ceremonially when Mary-the-Church herself submits to a kind of "canon law" (with all its possible ambiguities). In the Mass, the Church would later return God's gift to him in sacrifice, but only to receive it back from God, like Isaac—a gift with heightened potency. And in the same Mass the Church, which is impure because of us, her members, would be purified so as to be able to surrender herself to God with her Lord and her Head "for the life of the world", whose guilt she "redeems". And the whole existential dimension of this ecclesial sacrifice will remain concealed within the poor husk of a mere ceremony.

Into the midst of this concealing fog, however, the sun of the Spirit beams forth, and it reveals the transition, the qualitative newness to be found in the setting of the Old Testament and the rising of the New: the "Holy Spirit" was over Simeon; "to him it had been revealed by the Holy Spirit that he would not see death before he had seen the Messiah of the Lord." "He came in the Spirit to the temple," took the Child in his arms and sang the hymn of the Old Testament's dismissal as it is fulfilled by the New. A part of his song of praise, however, is the prophecy concerning the sign of scandal that the Son would set up, and concerning the sword that would consequently pierce the heart of the Mother. And the last glance which holy Israel casts into the future is able to penetrate to the bottom of the mystery: the Child is to be "a light of revelation to the Gentiles", breaking forth from the night of the Cross and of the Jews' rejection, and this light is seen as the double-yet-single light that comes from the sacrifice of Child and Mother, of Christ and the Church.

The new light derives from the lived sacrifice; at its very core it is the light of obedience to the will of the Father. This obedience consists of having put oneself at God's disposal with that exclusiveness which is expressed in the virginity of all three persons in the Holy Family and which results in a poverty which can sacrifice only two doves because it has let itself be robbed clean by both God and man. What Jesus' preaching will later formulate as the "evangelical counsels" is nothing other than that life form which was given us with the incarnation of the Son, a form after which every Christian in every state of life within the Church must pattern himself.

## 5
*And blessed is the fruit of your womb*

# JESUS

*whom you, O Virgin,*
*found again in the temple*

AFTER WHAT HAD HAPPENED in the temple twelve years before, one would almost think that the parents should have looked for the Child there in the first place. Had they not offered him as a gift to God? Had not the prophet told them that this was no casual sacrifice, but rather the definitive one? But the new thing that Jesus brings is so unique that we can be initiated into it only by himself, only by the experience that we have of him. And the first stage of this initiation will always be an "inability to understand" (Lk 2:50) what he is saying to us. He is truly "the Way" that every Christian—even Mary—must first *tread* in order to understand that he is the Truth and the Life.

And so they find him in the temple, a place that is God's and where one cannot dwell in a human way: it contains no dining table or bed. The place that God inhabits is a place uninhabitable for men. God's Son, however, will always dwell there because he rests on the will of the Father, which the Spirit shows him because in this human manner of obedience he continues doing what he has done from all eternity—being "with God", "reposing in the bosom of the Father" (Jn 1:2, 18). In strict logic, therefore, and by contrast to the birds, which have nests, and the foxes, which have lairs, on earth the Son will possess nothing upon which to lay his head. For the time being, as long as the temple stands, he will dwell within it, since the sanctuary is the symbolic house of God in the world. But of this sanctuary there will not remain stone upon stone. And then the Son, who does the Father's will on earth as in heaven, will be the sole temple of God in the world. He himself speaks about this in obscure words when he says that in three days he will raise up again this temple which men will tear down. But with the twelve-year-old Jesus, the New Covenant once again remains hidden in the Old. He shall be God's place in the world, and because he will distribute himself to the whole world eucharistically and his distributed Body will build up his Church, this place will be universally accessible—but accessible only in the celebration, in the remembering that makes present his death and his resurrection, his being lost and his being found again. It is there, in the mystery of the Three Days, that he will have to be sought, just as his Mother and his foster father find him after three days of fruitless seeking. He will have to be sought where he is not: in sinners, in those alienated from God, in his solidarity with his enemies, with those who are lost, in those places where on the third day he makes himself known.

"Why have you done this to us? See how your father and I have sought you with much suffering." He cannot spare them this pain. Only in his seeking can a Christian find, in a seeking so earnest that it would seem that absolutely everything depended on finding this sought-for thing. There is no prescription for Christian living other than this very graphic instruction: one will find Jesus only in the place where he has surrendered himself —and where man has delivered him—over to God. All Christians must first seek him "among acquaintances and relatives", up and down the world; but in the end one always hears from him the words: "Did you not know that I must be about my Father's business?" Like Mary and Joseph, we will probably not understand any of it at first, and we will be sent off on yet a longer way of search. The seeking can continue even after Easter. Mary Magdalen seeks for him in the grave, but after he lets himself be found she grasps at him as if he were a possession, and he withdraws. And in the same way, he withdraws from the sight of the disciples of Emmaus the moment they have found him. We find him definitively only in the place of the Father, in heaven, which is to say when finding no longer implies containing God within our space, but rather when it means that we have been found by God, that we have entered into his space, that we are "known by God" (1 Cor 13:12). "God is infinite so that we will continue to seek for him even after we have found him" (Augustine).

The more genuinely Christian a finding is, the more will it be an expropriation. The two phrases "your father and I" and "my Father" collide severely. Jesus cannot have two fathers. If Joseph were his physical father, Jesus would here be violating the fourth commandment; but he does not do this in any sense, since immediately he will "be subject to them". He is not an emancipated youth that assigns to himself a task in opposition to his parents, who fail to understand him. All he does is make manifest his truth: he is the Son of God, comparable to no one else, and the Son of a virginal Mother. As such a human son he is given back to them in their joy at having found him again. He is not merely given to them on loan; he is given back to them as gift, but with the injunction that they receive him as who he is in truth. With respect to God there can be no will-to-possession, since God himself has no desire to possess. Does he not give his Son away to all, irrevocably? Only in this way does he have him. No man can be rich in God if he does not want to partake of God's poverty.

Now that the Son returns to them, Mary and Joseph will have to learn what it means "to possess as if one did not possess" (1 Cor 7:30), to be ready at all times to let what one holds dearest pass over to the side of God and to let oneself be drawn along on this path of ravishment. In the Sermon on the Mount, Jesus will expressly demand the readiness to let oneself be despoiled: here again poverty and obedience are bound together. Since Mary still does "not understand", she will have to endure a harder loss: instead of three days it will later be three years. After his going forth, Jesus will not write home and send news about himself to his family. Indeed (and this is worse), he will not even receive those relatives who visit him. So much is he at home within the will of his Father that whoever wants to find him must go outside himself, follow after him, and do the will of his heavenly Father (Mk 3:31ff). While here in the temple she is the one who finds him, his Mother will afterwards serve as an object of demonstration: it is she who will be the most rejected, the most abandoned of all. And we are not told how much of all this she will "understand" during her years of solitude. Not to understand and yet to believe, not to understand and yet to assent is part of the very fiber of Christian faith. Even the Son himself on the cross will not understand why the Father has abandoned him. "What you fully understand cannot be God" (Augustine).

However: "He went down with them and came to Nazareth and was subject to them. His Mother kept all these words in her heart. And Jesus grew in wisdom and age and grace before God and men." The obedience which the Son will now give them for two decades is an obedience which has become man, an obedience existing within a human community, but one which always flows from his obedience to the Father, whose will introduces him to the sphere of this human obedience. One may and must order him about now. But here in Nazareth care has been taken that even the orders proceed from a knowledge of the divine will. And if he does grow in wisdom and age this is not least of all because of his incarnate obedience, which makes him grow more deeply into the will of the Father, who wants to make his Word penetrate down to the most material reality. He grows in age, and in this way the Incarnation continues its course. He grows in wisdom, because the Father initiates him, the obedient one, ever more deeply into the mystery which he himself is: God's Word within the form of a human life. He grows in grace, which refers not only to his being full of the Holy Spirit but also to his human goodness, affability, moral attractiveness. In this way something admirable is unfolding before his parents' eyes, something they contemplate and in which they are allowed to participate.

There are no valid excuses for refusing such gifts as God gives us in connection with his Son. Whatever he entrusts to us of what is his should occasion joy in us. There is no such thing as a joyless Christian; all interior nights presuppose a knowledge of the light, all sacrifices presuppose that something is possessed. The joy that is here given to Mary and Joseph is not merely supernatural: it is a thoroughly human joy, just as Jesus does not obey them merely for "supernatural motives" but out of a genuinely human love and respect. The supernatural virtues—such as faith, hope and love—that flow from God's inner life are intended to assume in Jesus' incarnation a truly human form. In the Holy Family such humanness is not a difficult thing.

But later on Mary will pass into the interior of the Church, and for the Church's sake as visible community a hierarchical authority will be instituted by Jesus himself in the name of his divine authority. When this happens, then obedience will have a harder time of it to retain its *charis*, the natural attractiveness of the human. At times a tension can even come into play between the ecclesial authority that exacts obedience and the divine authority which always must be obeyed. But the saints have withstood this tension without ever refusing the Church the obedience which is her due. It is a matter of patience, of waiting and trusting. Such tensions are a participation in the Incarnation of the Son, who had to experience in himself the tension between God and man, who had to "learn" (Heb 5:8) the tension between immediate obedience to the Father and the obedience to men which the Father demanded of him.

It goes without saying that the Church has the duty to train believers in the obedience which constitutes her own innermost mystery: she must train them, through their obedience to her, to attain to her obedience to God. The protracted example of Jesus fills the greater part of his life: he is obedient to Mary, and also to Joseph for as long as the latter lives. This experience on Jesus' part is in the first place an initiation to Mary's assent to God, until Mary, having become the Church, is herself drawn into her Son's divine and human obedience and, in Christ, becomes obedient to the Father. Every hierarchical office proceeds from personal love, but all personal love must allow itself to be expanded, beyond itself and its power of comprehension, by the objectivized form of love which is the hierarchical office. The Holy Spirit is both things in unity: both subjective and objective love, both felt and unfelt love, both familiarity and office, both inspiration and submission.

Mary keeps all these things in her heart. She lets them grow in her bosom in order afterwards to pass them on to the Church and her hierarchical institution as being the archetypal Christian experience and wisdom. In the course of her slow contemplation the things she does not understand begin to gain light, even though (or *because*) she will remain a striver all her life long. It is for just this reason that she is not fallible. The Church, consisting of sinners, will have to unite both things in a still more paradoxical fashion: on the one hand she is always under way, she has never arrived; on the other hand, she is the one who both knows the way and can show it to others. For Mary, Simeon's prophecy is an infallible road sign: as long as she is moving closer to this sword which is to pierce her heart, she knows that she is on the right road—that of her Son. Her being inspired in this way does not preclude her daily searching anew for her road in obedience. In this her search, which can never err, she is at the heart of the Church the example for the manner in which we can and should remain in the Church and, through her, on the way which is Christ.

# THE TRANSITION

*Like the Church year, the Rosary too passes from the cycle of feasts of the young Christ to the cycle of the Passion and that of its transfiguration from Easter to the Ascension. The Rosary, after all, is a prayer of Marian participation and mediation. The rejections of Mary by Christ during his public life had become a frequent theme toward the end of the cycle of Christ's youth. From Mary's viewpoint this means that, for her, the Passion had already begun. When the Passion now becomes the central subject contemplated by our prayer, we see that, in the Passion, the Son finds himself in solitude, and consequently, so does the Mother. Not even her standing under the cross or her being entrusted to John is explicitly mentioned. And yet, during the Passion and Mary's hidden participation in it, there takes place her decisive transformation into the Church* as Bride of the Lord. *The sword pierces her soul and bares it, "that the thoughts of many hearts may be revealed" (Lk 2:35): this baring penetration of her heart is like the echo within the Church of the stroke of the lance, of the blood and the water and the Eucharist. Mary's word of assent flows out at this moment, as it were, and it becomes accessible to all who to any degree would like to say yes. It cannot be otherwise: what, by her anticipated consent, became the embryo of Christ's body, now itself becomes expanded along with the colossal expansion of God's Word upon the cross, where the incarnation is consummated. And this does not occur as a second principle, autonomous from the first, which is the Son's atoning suffering: the Mother's suffering grows along with the Son's, just as the echo grows with the shout. Indeed, Mary's word of assent had from the outset been the reverberation of the eternal word of assent which the Son gives in heaven to the Father's trinitarian decision to save mankind.*

*This is why, beyond all the compassion we naturally can feel for the Mother's suffering, the most rigorous theology demands of us that we pray to her and beg for admission into her open heart. It is through her that we will come to participate in the interior space of her Son's suffering, which is almost inaccessible to us in our sinfulness.*

*And blessed is the fruit of your womb*

JESUS

*who sweated blood for us*

IMPORTANT AS THE ACTIONS, teachings and mira-
cles of Jesus' public life were and remain, they
are but the entrance into and the beginning of his
decisive deed: the gathering up into himself of the
world's sin, which offends the goodness of the
Father, in order to burn it utterly in the fire of his
suffering. The Father is henceforth to perceive this
sin as being only fuel for the Son's love: "Behold
the Lamb of God [the scapegoat], who takes away
the sin of the world [into the desert, into a place
which is out of sight and unreachable]." Now that
the Son has admitted sin's monstrous darkness
into himself, he is as if robbed of his power: he
has "emptied himself out" in order to bear the
unbearable burden in a weakness that makes the
task before him an utterly overtaxing prospect. At

the time of his temptation in the wilderness all the world's enticements—those of an easy road that attracts men—clearly ran counter to the Father's will. And this will could triumph in him because the Father ever appeared before his soul as being the ever-greater and adorable reality. Now the temptation is quite different. The choice is not between the Father and the world, but between two images of the Father. On the one hand, there is the God who is known to be almighty and all-good from all time and before the present interior darkness Jesus experiences; this God could have selected for him wholly different paths to arrive at the same goal. On the other hand, there is the inexorable God of justice, which is how the Father now appears to the Son, since he is seeing him and experiencing him through the heart and the eyes of sinners. The sun of love has disappeared behind the clouds; only the threat of the divine thunderstorm can be perceived. This situation belongs to the triune plan of salvation, but the Son is now in his totality the Man Who Bears Sin, and the Holy Spirit now presents the Father's will to him only as the manifest contradiction between a person whose essence it is to be imposed upon and a person who does nothing but overexact.

In his frightful anguish of not being equal to

what is demanded, he must see his way clear to his word of assent. It is truly a wrestling match with himself; he must struggle until he produces the "Thy will be done" by overstraining in uttermost darkness. This is proven by the words concerning his "sweat of blood", words that many copyists have omitted but which are a part of the genuine text of the Gospel. Neither the sleeplessness that Jesus demands ("watch and pray") nor the purely human fear and agitation at the imminent suffering can explain this eruption of his innermost substance; it can be explained only in terms of a conflict which is waged between the God who is in heaven and the God who is on earth substituting for sinners.

We read that Jesus interrupted this struggle several times to look for sympathy, support and help in his disciples. They are the representatives of the visible Church, ranked by the Lord himself in a certain order. Eight of them stand further back, and three more in the foreground, closer to Jesus, apparently to have some share in the events. We see their failure; they sleep for sheer sadness, for desperate confusion, but also because of a failure in their obedience, which cannot utter the "yes" of faith to the bitter end, which is not watchful and prayerful enough. This is the Church as we ordinarily encounter her, especially when in

73

the three closer disciples we see the representatives of those who are particularly chosen to live the life of the counsels and of the priesthood: from these a more rigorous obedience in faith is demanded than from the rest. It is as if the rest uttered a general consent, one which is a bit too abstract, an assent to the faith of the Church and to her most important instructions; but they do not live within the daily tested form of a concrete obedience to a superior or to a bishop. The disciples lag behind their own calling; they leave the Lord alone.

He must return to the thick of his solitary battle, which does not seem to progress but always stands at the same point of unsurpassable impotence. He prays "with the same words", even if "the more ardently". In the battle of obedience no progress need be felt. Matters can be quite the opposite, in fact. As time goes on, God can burden us even more severely, and the stages of difficulty can become even more precarious due to the fact that, unbeknownst to us, we have indeed been learning all along. The things that interest God about our obedience are not those that seem easy to us but those that are difficult. Like an engineer with a new bridge, God has to conduct load tests with man.

The representatives of the official Church did not produce the expected echo; the Head's loud "yes" did not penetrate down into the Body. But before the outbreak of his suffering he did encounter that loving woman who anointed him with uncalculating lavishness and whose action he defended before the irate disciples. The fragrance of her ointment filled the whole house. "Allow her," said Jesus, "she has anointed me with reference to my burial." It is as if from this Mary there had resounded an extravagant word of self-surrendering consent that represents a genuine echo of the Son's assent to his suffering. It is a consent which fully accepts the Passion of the Beloved, and this is more difficult than assuming the hardest suffering oneself.

This Mary, with her visible gesture, is like an image of the final fidelity which was active invisibly in the Mother's word of assent. For it is the Mother's consent which is immaculate and, hence, fundamentally without bounds—even if it is a consent which is uttered in just as boundless an exhaustion and a powerlessness. It is something which now must be snatched from her, torn from her, something which she can no longer herself pray, but which is a prayer that God himself must shape from her substance. "Holy Mary, Mother of God, pray for us sinners," not with words but with your very being.

## 2

*And blessed is the fruit of your womb*

## JESUS

*who was scourged for us*

T HE IMPRISONMENT, the hearings and the con-
demnation have already taken place when
Jesus is led to the whipping post. The consequences of the greatest misjudgment in human
history begin to take effect. For here all of mankind is gathered. First of all, the Christians—those
who know what is at stake: Judas betrayed him
and in this way triggered the Passion; Peter denied
him contrary to his promise, and that of all the
others, to follow him to the point of death; most
of them have fled cowardly. The Jews to whom
Jesus was handed over want to know nothing of
such a Messiah; he does not correspond to the
chimera of worldly power they envision; unlike
Abraham, they are no longer open to being led by
God but have carved for themselves an idol out of
their own wishful thinking: "We have no king but

Caesar." Thus Jesus is cast out to the pagans, who cannot possibly know his being and his mission: "What is truth?"

And all want to disentangle themselves from the clinging guilt. Judas gives back the blood money. The Jews hesitate to put it in the temple treasury. Pilate washes his hands in innocence. No one wants to be the one. No one thinks of God; all fling his fatherly goodness back in his face precisely when he offers men his most precious possession with open hands. The stroke against God's hand hits what it contains, hits it with a shower of blows by which mankind lets God know what it thinks of him. This is man's memorandum to God.

Why was Jesus scourged? Certainly not because Pilate was making one last effort to soften the Jews. And also not in order to extort from Jesus a confession by means of torture: he had already confessed. Rather, this is a preparatory measure for the crucifixion. The Jews scourged with a certain restraint: forty strokes less one—out of compassion. Pagan soldiers (scourging was primarily a military punishment) often thrashed their victim to death, with sophisticated instruments whose straps were provided with bits of bone or lead which often succeeded in exposing the internal organs. It is possible that a company of

Syrians—whose particular hatred for the Jews was known—was charged with the ordeal, during which they were free to vent their mockery on Jesus.

What God the Father is holding in his hand is the Lamb of God, which takes upon itself the sin of the world, truly and bodily. What is involved here is a kind of perverse sacrament that effects interiorly what it signifies in the external image: the sufferings which are being driven into the body of Jesus are in truth the sins of the world, knocked forcibly into his total divine and human person. It is not only man who is a whole: his spirit feels what is done to his body. The God-man, too, is indivisible: in his humanity God experiences what the sin of the world is. It is an incalculably amorphous amalgam, which at the same time contains the sin of every individual human being in infinite differentiation. It contains my sins, too, which in turn are innumerable. If a sin, which is a palpable reality, is remitted by absolution, it does not simply dissolve into nothingness: through the alchemy of divine love it dissolves into the suffering of Christ. God, says Paul, "made him who knew nothing of sin to be sin for us" (2 Cor 5:21), which means both things: that he was made the personification of the world's sin and the "sin offering" to expiate it.

At the scourging it is not an ordinary physical suffering which is administered to the God-Man, but a suffering which could only take place in him, which can only be borne by him. And it is only by taking us up in this corporeal way into his flesh and blood that he can then communicate to us this flesh and blood as being our incarnate reconciliation: the "Body delivered over for us" and the "Blood poured out for us", as the words of consecration say. In its totality, Christianity never ceases being Incarnation: God's incarnation in Christ, the incarnation of sin in Christ, and Christ's incarnation in our corporeal existence. The Holy Spirit is never a spirit of disembodiment: it is he who always holds before the Son the Father's will that he should venture forth to the "lowermost regions" of material cosmos (cf. Eph 4:9). Whoever strives upward toward God must, at the same time, let God show him the way down: he must go from mere ideas and concepts to reach a truth that pierces through bone and marrow, there to sink its roots.

The body that takes upon itself the sin of the world is a "fruit of your body", as the Hail Mary prays. Now, this origin is not a merely physiological event which then vanishes into the past; it is an event that concerns the ever-present fruitfulness of faith. For this reason, the Mother's body cannot help but feel what is done to her "fruit". Because in a mysterious way Mary communes with the sufferings of her Son, she experiences in her own manner what is the sin of the world. Being sinless, she has no direct contact with the world's sin, but she recognizes its true reality reflected in the body of her Son, where sin, which in itself is always a lie and a mask, shows its real face. Paul can say that he suffers for the Church in his body what is still lacking to the sufferings of Christ (Col 1:24). So, if the Lord reserves for his chosen ones a sphere of co-suffering within his own all-sufficient suffering, how much more will this not hold for the "pure and immaculate Bride, the Church" (Eph 5:27) herself, who is such originally only in Mary, and who, precisely as bride, constitutes "one flesh" (Eph 5:31) with her Bridegroom? And we must reflect that "this is a great mystery" also (and especially) in the context of the Passion.

It goes without saying that, even as one redeemed in advance, Mary is not a "redemptrix" on an equal footing with her Son. If this were so she would have redeemed herself. Her role is always that of one who assents to whatever God wants to do, even when this is most incomprehensible to her. Hers is a consent which is constantly being expanded wider and wider. Here in the

Passion she is being asked that, for the sake of God and that of man, she say yes to the unimaginable torture of her Child. This is more horrible for her than if she were herself to suffer.

## 3
*And blessed is the fruit of your womb*

# JESUS

*who was crowned with thorns for us*

A FTER THE FLOGGING comes the grandly staged
and diabolically conceived mockery: royal
mantle, scepter, crown, genuflection and words
of homage. God is at the same time recognized
and rejected by the *homme révolté*; without this
recognition the blasphemy would wholly lose its
edge.

Seen from the outside the scenes of the Passion
succeed one another, always showing new aspects
of the work of salvation. But for the suffering
Jesus everything is present at once: everything is
betrayal, everything is deliverance into suffering,
everything brings anguish and insult, everything
is his assumption of sins, everything is the mas-
querade of his derision. . . . Neither sin nor the
redemption can be neatly divided. There was

83

scorn already in Judas' kiss, and scorn will, to the very end, make its way up to the Crucified. In the miserable figure that is dressed up as a king, the world derides the God who appears to be too weak to manifest his divinity in the world; and at the same time the world is deriding itself, since in this way its contemptibleness becomes isolated as such and is thus brought into the light. "His appearance was inhumanly distorted, and his figure was no longer that of the children of men. . . . He was despised, like one before whom people cover their face; he was detested, regarded by no one" (Is 52:14; 53:3). Even his fellow sufferers mock him. In Mark and Matthew both thieves join in the accusing tirades of the mockers. Is not the world's suffering the best occasion to raise an accusing fist against God?

Mocked is the majesty that had become manifest to all, both to the people and to his powerful opponents. Jesus never showed himself other than in this majesty, whether he appeared with his fullness of power ("But I say to you. . . .") or revealed himself in his meekness as the Son of Man who is humble of heart. His was a divine majesty that exposed itself wholly unprotected, so that it elicited both scandal and aggression. The fact that he never struck back when attacked only made his majesty radiate all the more brightly, but it also enticed some to concoct plans for his defeat. The provocation effected by his majesty put before people the choice that John formulates as follows: "I have not come to judge the world but to save the world. Whoever rejects me and does not accept my words has his judge: the Word that I have spoken will judge him on the Last Day" (Jn 12:47f). The inexorable necessity of making a choice is founded on the fact that Jesus exposes himself so defenselessly, not for his own sake, but for the sake of God the Father, for the absolute love of the primal Source. Through his majestic lowliness the primal Light becomes visible. Whoever does not want to see and to admit this must have previously withdrawn into positions of earthly power: politics, the use of violence, liquidation —*previously*, I say, when it was not yet possible merely to ignore him as it is today, when one could not yet drown his uniqueness in a sea of quantity and pluralism. And since he does not defend himself against all this in the Father's hour, his Passion becomes a triumphant procession of Jews and pagans parading by him. Now it is they who are the provocateurs. "Prophesy, prophet! Who is it that struck you?" "Physician, heal yourself!" "If you are the Messiah, the Son of God, come down from the cross!"

The King's crown is pressed into his head until

it has become anchored in flesh and bone. The thorns of contempt lodge deep. These thorns represent everything that rejects the God of majestic humiliation, the God who washes feet, the God who squanders himself in the Eucharist. It could be religion as a work of self-perfectioning or as a bulwark erected against God, or religion as ritualism and mere tradition, as bourgeois convention or as magic. It could be a godlessness that oscillates between the Eastern and Western extremes, either as denial of the world or as materialistic communism, with all their possible variations. In every case what is involved is the world as self-sufficient, a world for which God, in the event that he does exist, is but a means to its own goals.

During his public life Jesus had rejected the royal dignity (Jn 6:15); now, when he is delivered over to the worldly powers that "have an abysmal hatred against him" (Jn 15:25), the word "king" is heard again. "Yes, I am a king," says Jesus to Pilate, at once accepting and refuting the accusation of the Jews. And this remains inscribed above his head in the world's universal languages while, below, he is dying. Only here, in the midst of mockery and extinction, is this title of honor fully his; we cannot celebrate "Christ the King" independently of this situation, which is where his kingship fully emerges. It is not after the Cross, when he is elevated by God, that the one who until now had been God's Servant becomes the Ruler: it is in the Passion that his kingliness, which had always been latent, becomes fully revealed. Adoration is here taking place: the cohort adores by means of its carnival farce; the believers adore when in the *Ecce Homo* they recognize the *Ecce Deus*, at once the most hidden and the most manifest image of divine love (*Adoro te devote, latens Deitas, quae sub his figuris vere latitas*); God the Father himself adores when in his Son's deed he sees realized the boldest designs of his love. Why should the divine Persons not adore one another, since each of them is God in just as fundamental a way, and each in a manner which is inimitable and incomparable to the other two? How should the Holy Spirit not admire with adoration what he has received from the Father to present to the Son, not admire what the Son with the power of his divine and human inventiveness has brought to the utmost possible realization?

But: "Remember my word to you: the servant is not above his Lord; if they have persecuted me they will also persecute you" (Jn 15:20). "The disciple can be happy when things go for him as they do for his Master, and the slave when things go for him as they do for his Lord" (Mt 10:25). In the first place we must here think of the Mother before we move on to the Apostles and their successors and all believers to whom the Lord's exhortation is addressed. Mary, too, wears her invisible crown of thorns, woven not only from the derision of her Son but also from all the contempt heaped on her own majesty: that she bore a son to Joseph, for instance, not to say an illegitimate son; that she has fostered a cult to herself which obscures the cult due her Son; that she has adorned herself with the attributes of the pagan goddesses Ishtar and the Magna Mater in order to exert on the Christian people a seductive influence. . . . Even Catholics maintain an embarrassed silence in her regard. Pagans, Jews and Christians have made her to be the *Mater Dolorosa*. When prayed to this Mother, the Hail Mary now acquires a new sound.

Only in the end, and then only in utter unworthiness and encouraged by Jesus' word, may we place ourselves on the side of the Mother who is so unjustly despised. "If they call the head of the house Beelzebub, how much more the members of his household!" (Mt 10:25); how much more, not because the name would be given to them even more unjustly, but on the contrary, because they have deserved it in so many respects. How seldom can the Church look on herself as being persecuted unjustly! "Blessed are you when they insult you and persecute you and utter every kind of slander against you because of me" (Mt 5:11). But when are they really lying? The Church has sins stretching over centuries for which a later generation will justly have to suffer even though it can do nothing about them. And if a thorn from the Lord's crown should be bored into our forehead or our neck we will at once think it some misunderstanding, and when we feel it reaching more deeply we will pray: "Lord, I am not worthy."

## 4

*And blessed is the fruit of your womb*

# JESUS

*who bore the heavy cross for us*

For us: These two words occur in every mystery of the present cycle and we will here consider them expressly This "for us" is the first and fundamental word of Christian faith, the root from which has developed the entire tree of the Creed and of dogmatics. For us did Jesus become man, for us and because of our sins did he die and rise: and if he was able to do this, then from the very outset he was "truly the Son of God" (Mk 15:39). He can introduce us into his eternal life, and all judgment of the world and of mankind in truth belongs to him. Already at his conversion Paul found this "for us" in the faith of the primitive community, and he took it up to develop it further.

It is in this that the Christian principle is radically different from all other religions and world views; it is here that its uniqueness lies. In the great religions of the East each person lives for himself and looks after himself, strives for his own liberation from the world's suffering and has his own techniques to achieve this. A handful can actually follow these techniques with rigor; the majority, in order to be able to live, must work out compromises, and they have a multitude of rites and customs that compensate for this. People pray much, undertake much, renounce much, but each one has only his own salvation in mind. There is, indeed, talk of compassion, but this compassion can never become transformed into an effective substitution for others. Even Amida, the mediator of salvation who may be invoked, cannot himself forgive sin by dissolving it in the pain of a divine and human suffering.

It may happen that one sacrifices himself for a group, which always has preponderance over the individual. A soldier, for instance, may sacrifice himself in war for his people. Great tragedies glorify such sacrifices, especially when they have occurred willingly. Or a person may sacrifice his life for his convictions, for his faith (as Socrates did): this is the most spiritual deed that a human being can perform. In this way he becomes an example for many, but he cannot interiorly communicate to others his own sacrificial power. In rare cases, says Paul (Rom 5:7), someone may sacrifice himself for a beloved friend, in order to save his physical life: more is not possible. But who would ever surrender his physical and spiritual life for people who are his enemies? And who could do it efficaciously for all of humanity, in the name of a God who is ignored and hated, fully empowered by this God to do so, not out of a divine tyranny seeking in this way to restore its injured honor, but rather out of the common understanding of a love that presupposes, precisely, the mystery of God's triunity? There must exist the free offer of a love that seeks to reconcile the world with God: we find this in the Son. There must exist a mandate that freely allows this to be done in obedience: we find this in the Father. There must exist the indissoluble unity of these two freedoms: this is the Spirit. And finally, there must exist the possibility of doing this effectively: this is the Son's incarnation, which is the prerequisite for the "wondrous exchange" (*admirabile commercium*) between sin that is borne and grace that is communicated. And in this exchange one last thing is required: the agreement of "us" for whom the God-man suffers: this is Mary's word of assent, spoken in place of all those others who cannot yet utter it, for otherwise the act of Christ's substitution for us would not only remain one-sided, but indeed exterior.

Only this whole context makes evident that the Way of the Cross that now begins is a way full of meaning for us, that it is indeed the only way that begins to give meaning to our whole existence. It means that the inconceivable burden of this world —everything in the world which is evil, unjust, cruel, destructive of hope—does not necessarily crush the pitiful fellow who undertakes to load it alone on his own shoulders. It means that there exists a counterweight of a wholly different order, because the weight of this defenseless, self-surrendering love is not measurable as it undertakes to remove the sin of the world by allowing its forces to be taxed to the utmost.

What this burden is in truth no man will ever be able to measure, for it is precisely the burden which has been taken from him. At most we have a dark inkling that for our failures—both the partial and the total—we will have to atone, but how much is what we do not dare to think through. In the end we do not even need to visualize it in its entirety, not only because this would not lead anywhere, but above all because the burden has already been borne. This is not a quantity which could be calculated—the individual's weight of sin multiplied by billions. No road leads from this to what really is essential. What is involved here is, above all, a quality which can only be experienced by the one who has loaded upon himself its most fundamental trait: the contradiction between the God of love and the hatred and indifference of the world. As we adore the mystery of how our burden has been borne for us, the most we can do is formulate the resolution to be willing to bear what is given us to bear. For the most part this is precisely what we do not like to bear and what perhaps we would by all means like to reject as unbearable. By sheer force of being overtaxed in this way we at times arrive at the borderline beyond which lies the Country of the Cross, the Land of Exorbitant Demand.

Toward the end of the *Rule of Saint Benedict* the question is asked as to what a person must do when impossible things (*impossibilia*) are demanded of him. Already in earlier times the old abbots and fathers of the desert, to whom disciples flocked, watched for an opportunity themselves to do impossible things in their imitation of Christ and to expect the same from others. Benedict, and Ignatius after him, are gentler: whoever thinks that something imposed on him surpasses his strength should say so to the abbot, and if the abbot insists on what he has commanded, the person should nonetheless try to do it. This is very

95

close to the scene we witness on the Mount of Olives: "If this cup could pass from me, . . . but your will be done." Christ's suffering, his bearing of the cross, appears from the outset to be an impossible thing because it surpasses all human power. Whoever has the feeling that he can overcome such a situation with his own powers is not yet on the Way of the Cross.

Although Jesus is alone on the Way of the Cross, he moves forward surrounded by a mass of people. And there are not only onlookers among them but also followers. There is that Simon of Cyrene who is coerced to carry the cross—probably one of the two beams—in place of Jesus. The Gospel here makes an astounding double affirmation. John insists on the fact that "Jesus carried his cross himself" (Jn 19:17); and the Synoptics expressly describe for us the person of Simon, who is forced to take up the beam. At a deeper level both things are equally true: that the Son of God alone bears the whole guilt of the world since only he can bear it, and that he nevertheless leaves open a certain sphere where others may bear it with him. It is not at all as if anyone could "co-redeem" on the same level as he. But in the most solitary of tasks an element of human community is needed, at least in the form of tacit agreement. Paul is aware of the paradox of this manner of presence: on the one hand, he says concerning himself that he has been crucified with Jesus and that he bears his wounds (Gal 2:19; 6:17); on the other hand, he is enraged at the thought that his suffering could be compared to that of Christ: "Has perhaps Paul been crucified for you?" (1 Cor 1:13).

More deep than Simon's, who unwillingly helps with the carrying, more deep than Paul's, who oscillates vehemently between being attracted to and repulsed by the Cross, is the suffering of Mary as she follows the Cross-bearer. In her spirit she suffers from not being able to relieve her Son of any suffering. She must leave the entire burden to him, whom the scourging has already debilitated almost to the point of death, and Mary darkly knows that this burden exceeds all the world's weights. She has to let it happen, and can only offer him this *letting happen* which as such cannot accomplish anything. But this is not for her an occasion of despair, because her thoughts do not dwell on her own ability or inability, but wholly on her Son. And she does not stage a revolt either against God, who allows these things to happen, or against mankind, which is torturing her Son. She lets it all happen in the context of a consent which no longer has any active power, but which is like an infinite—eucharistic—dissolution.

Nothing is reported to us about an encounter between Mother and Son on the Way of the Cross, not even a spot of comfort such as provided by the tale of the compassionate Veronica. The weeping women of Jerusalem are rebuffed: there is no place here for professional mourners. The Mother has vanished anonymously somewhere in the crowd along with the Beloved Disciple. Through the ages it is always so for those who are admitted to the way of discipleship in the holy Church.

## 5
### *And blessed is the fruit of your womb*

# JESUS

### *who was crucified for us*

T HE DEEPER THE SUFFERING BECOMES, the more
our concepts fail to grasp it. Every word is
silenced before this last station, when God's living
Word is nailed by men into deathly immobility. It
is the Father's hour, when the eternal triune plan is
executed to clear out all the refuse of the world's
sin by burning it in the fire of suffering love. This
fire has burned eternally in God as the blazing
passion that is always intent on the eternal good,
in which God's counsel has decided that the world
too should participate. This good is the resolute
commitment of the divine Persons to one another,
the triune radicalism which here reaches out to
include the world. The mystery of the Cross is the
supreme revelation of the Trinity.

The begetting of the Son goes to the point of his

being freely given away; the relationship of the Outflow with its Source appears to be interrupted; the concentration of all that is ungodly in the Son is experienced by him as his abandonment by the Father. The wellspring from which the Son eternally lives appears to have dried up, and with this, everything the Son has done purely on mandate from the Father loses its meaning; it has been in vain. What gives the Son this feeling is by no means only the earthly fiasco of his life's end; at a much deeper level it is the necessity of bearing interiorly the irreconcilable contradiction between the sin which he has within himself and the loving Father's will to save. As the very embodiment of sin he can no longer find support in God; he has identified himself with what God must eternally reject from himself. And yet he is the Son, who can only proceed and live from the source that is the Father, and this is the reason for his infinite thirst for the inaccessible Father. It is a thirst which burns in him like an eternal fire—physical, psychic, spiritual. The Holy Spirit, who throughout his earthly life has accompanied him as the Spirit of the Father, is nothing now but the kindler of this thirst: he unites Father and Son by wrenching apart their reciprocal love to an unbearable degree. In this infinite difference between Father and Son two things are revealed: the infinite difference within God himself, which is the presupposition for divine love and is bridged over in the Holy Spirit, and their difference within salvation history, whereby the alienated world is reconciled with God.

In this the Cross is the dramatic about-face from the old to the new. This means not only a turning away from the Old Testament (in which we heard so much of God's wrath and fury, of his bloody winepress), but a turning away from the whole of the decaying old world; and it is not only a turning to the Church (which will be the visible sacrament of reconciliation with God), but to the whole of the new world which is here being born and which is to be perfected at creation's final transfiguration. The Cross is the turning point, the transition, the Passover. And in the turning point—in the Crucified—both things coincide: God's fury, which will make no compromises with sin but can only reject it and burn it to ashes, and God's love, which begins to reveal itself precisely at the place of this inexorable confrontation.

It is as such a turning point that the Crucified is the Word which the Father addresses to the world. At this moment the Word cannot hear itself. It shatters in the cry for the lost God. And when the Evangelists attain to such formulations as "Forgive them. . . ", "Today you will be with me in paradise", and "It is consummated", they are interpreting for us the full heavenly meaning of the Word on the Cross, as if these statements were the very voice of the Father and the Spirit in the Son. We may legitimately receive these words as spoken to us by the Father through the Spirit in the suffering of the Son.

But we are initiated into still more. At the heart of this turning point lies the Church's hour of birth; the Body of God's Word—immersed to the end in the divine fullness (Col 2:9), but also in the substance of the world which it has assumed—can now be distributed eucharistically, and from the pierced Heart there run out the water and blood of the sacraments. In the midst of this great event, this Body cannot forget its origin and its connection with its Mother's body. And the body of Jesus' Mother could bear this fruit only because she had consented in advance to Jesus' whole mission; this is why Mary is present under the cross at the moment when God's incarnation is consummated and the Church is born. She suffers along with her Son; in her spirit she experiences his death, and the stroke of the lance that pierces the dead Jesus' heart wounds her, who must survive him, as the sword that had been promised. The disciples have already communicated in the Eucharist; sacramentally they are already Christ's

Body; objectively, the Church which they constitute is already with Jesus on the cross. But sub-
jectively they are absent—except for the Beloved
Disciple, who represents them all.

The Crucified utters a word whereby he entrusts Mary to the Disciple as his mother and the
Disciple to Mary as her son, and this word in a
way constitutes the Church's foundation docu-
ment, flowing out of the midst of the suffering
which gives birth to the Church as such. Mary,
who is the *Immaculata Ecclesia* (Eph 5:27), the
heavenly Church who is perfected in advance, is
infused into the form of the earthly, organized
Church, and to this latter there are entrusted the
care and protection of the purity and sanctity of
the original—the ideal—Church. In the future,
both of them will belong together as strictly as
Mary and Jesus were—and remain—"one flesh".
And John is there representing Peter and the whole
group of the Twelve, as the last chapter of his
Gospel unmistakably shows. In this way the unity
of Jesus is maintained uninterruptedly—starting
from Jesus himself, passing through Mary and
John, and reaching the visible form of the universal Church. In her totality, the universal Church is
the Body of Christ under the Head, and she owes
her very existence to the suffering of the Head.
Just as the unity of the Body may not be disrupted

horizontally (into different churches and sects), neither may it be disrupted vertically by separating the Church from Christ or even from Mary, or by suppressing the mediating role which the Beloved Disciple plays between Peter and Mary. For her part, Mary stands under the cross in a company of believing women, both named and unnamed, who in turn represent an aspect of the Church—of a corporeal Church that has participated in the experience of the Cross and which, as such, has been entrusted to the care of the hierarchical Church.

The mysteries of the Passion culminate in the cry of the God-forsaken Jesus on the cross and in his plunge into the night of a sinner's death. It is doubtless these mysteries which form the "sorrowful garland". If we were to look back to the mysteries of the Source, however, we would see that they already stood in the fore-shadow of suffering: they are a "joyful garland" only if the redeeming grace is received and assented to in advance, by anticipation of the Cross. Even at the outset there had been enough renunciations and abandonments! And if we were to look ahead at the third "glorious garland", we would see that it reveals only what was already contained in the Cross in a hidden way: God's victory over our sin in the Body of Jesus Christ and in the accompanying, co-suffering body of his Mother. And it is impossible to understand the glory to come other than as the majestic splendor of the Love that was crucified once and for all.

# THE CONSUMMATION

*And blessed is the fruit of your womb*

JESUS

*who rose from the dead*

If CHRIST DID NOT RISE then our faith is empty (1 Cor 15:14). Without the Resurrection there would be no evangelical witness; Jesus' whole life, even his Passion, was composed for the sake of this witness about the Resurrection and its light. The disciples' ready avowal that, before the Resurrection, they had not understood everything decisive, the portrayal of their unbelief even with regard to the fact of the Resurrection, the total about-face of a Mary Magdalen, or of the disciples of Emmaus, or of a Paul: all of this belongs to the Easter proclamation.

The Resurrection is a trinitarian event. With his death on the cross, the Son of God fulfilled his mandate; with his human spirit he gave back to the Father also the Holy Spirit of his mission. As a man he cannot himself rise from the dead; it is the Father who, as "the God of the living" (Rom 4:17), awakens the Son from among the dead so that he, as one freshly united with the Father, can send forth God's Spirit into the Church.

Without the Resurrection the whole trinitarian plan of salvation would be incomprehensible, and the work begun in the life of Jesus would remain meaningless. To the world, and also the Old Testament, Jesus' life was one continual provocation, since he raised himself above the authority of the law as its very goal and meaning. Imitating Abraham's blind faith, Israel must allow itself to be stretched out beyond itself if it is going to attain to fulfillment. And already at the beginning of Jesus' preaching it becomes clear that this is something Israel does not want. Jesus knew what his provocative task had to bring him, and with a steadfast countenance he moved on toward his death. The disciples follow full of fright (Mk 10:32), and this fright remains in their very limbs even at the Resurrection (Mk 16:8; Lk 24:22, 37). They have no preliminary notion of what a "resurrection" could be—not "on the Last Day" but right in the middle of their own time. That even in his suffering, Jesus overcame the world, even the future of the world; that for him the Last Day has already arrived, while the disciples still abide within time; these things could dawn on them only gradually. And it will be even more difficult for them to understand that henceforth the whole life of the Church was to retain the imprint of the double-yet-single event of Cross and Easter. In order to understand this, indeed, in order to live it, they had to become participants in the Spirit of Christ, who at the same time is the Spirit of the Father who designs and executes all divine plans.

But to receive the Spirit of Christ and of the Father at the same time means to partake in God's essential gift: the Body and Blood of the Son, which the Father holds out to the world through the Spirit's power of actualization. The reception of the Spirit and of the Eucharist are two sides of the same thing. Precisely when Jesus emphasizes with greatest urgency the absolute necessity of eating his Flesh and drinking his Blood (Jn 6:53), he adds: "It is the Spirit that gives life; the flesh is of no use" (Jn 6:63). From the instant the Spirit accompanied the Son's incarnation and, in the Son, may in a way be said to have "experienced" the world, the Spirit remains forever inseparable from flesh and blood. This is why the Church assembled at Easter encounters a Spirit-filled but also corporeal Christ: he breathes his Spirit into them (Jn 20:22), but he also wants to be touched by them so that no one will think that he is "a spirit" (Lk 24:39). And after the Ascension the Church will await both things: the promised Holy Spirit and the returning Lord, whose arrival she anticipates according to his command in the celebration of the breaking of the bread. The testimony which the disciples receive and are to hand on is complete, according to John, only when "water (Baptism), blood (the Eucharist) and Spirit" are found together (1 Jn 5:7). The encounter with the Lord at Easter must lead to the reception of the Spirit, so that the Lord is recognized and so that he can send forth the one who recognizes him: possession of the Spirit empowers one to do nothing other than proclaim and attest the fact that God the Father has given us his Son, who died and rose for us.

Henceforth the Church is what was created on the Cross: the gathering of believers around those who have been established in hierarchical offices, with Mary in their midst. Without any doubt it was to her, as the very core of the Church, that the Son first appeared (Ignatius of Loyola, *Spiritual Exercises*, no. 299). It was she who, before anyone else, was visited by the Spirit and conceived the Body of the Word. Crowding around Mary, the Church prays that the same thing might happen to her as happened in Mary her archetype. And Mary herself prays anew for this event; now she prays *as* the Church, as the central point in the Community of Saints, that the Word's incarnation, perfected in the Cross and the Resurrection, may be communicated to the whole community.

If we look ahead at the fulfillment of this prayer, as narrated by the Acts of the Apostles and as continued in the totality of the history of the Church, two things become clear: that the Holy Spirit is always coming anew, and that he is always placing the witnessing Church anew under the sign of Jesus Christ, which is to say a sign of humiliation, persecution—the Cross. The Acts of the Apostles is full, on the one hand, of the persecution of the Church: the Apostles are flogged, Peter is imprisoned, James murdered, Paul is chosen for a suffering which receives dramatic portrayal toward the end of the book; on the other hand, however, it is full of the Church's triumphal procession "from Jerusalem to Samaria and to the ends of the earth." Both things belong together; the first aspect is the sign for the genuineness and credibility of the second. In the end Paul walks the way of Christ in an exemplary manner: he is delivered over to the Jews by his Christian brethren, and by the Jews over to the pagans; and his road to Rome brings him to a mighty shipwreck. This coincides perfectly with the fact that Paul's Gospel is that of the Christ who rose definitively after being crucified: "The Lord is the Spirit" (2 Cor 3:17), and "death no longer has any power over him" (Rom 6:9).

With this the incomprehensible paradox of the Christian life comes fully to light: namely, that the Christian must daily take up his cross in order to rise anew daily with the dead Lord, "For while we live we are always being given up to death for Jesus' sake, so that the life of Jesus may be manifested in our mortal flesh" (2 Cor 4:11). Neither does the Church die only in an earthly and historical manner in order to rise up into a pure life in the beyond, nor does the Church move, in an earthly-historical sense, into a life of pure resurrection for which the Cross is only a means for self-development. The first of these things would be a denial of the Incarnation; the second would be a lapse back into (secularized) Old Testament hope. In all reality, Easter occurs on earth, but it does not lead away from the Cross but always to it. The whole Pasch—the whole passing-over from death to life—is a perennially present reality.

## 2

*And blessed is the fruit of your womb*

JESUS

*who ascended into heaven*

THE SON'S DESCENT from the divine nature into the form of a servant (Phil 2:7) must have a definite goal; this is his elevation by the Father above all the powers of the world on account of his having fulfilled his mission (Phil 2:9ff). His descent had been no mere spatial event, but something far deeper: out of (divine) obedience he had subjected himself to (human) obedience. And now his ascent is the revealing proclamation that this obedience had been nothing but pure freedom and love, and that now its fruitfulness is coming to light. For not in vain did God send his Word into the world, but rather in order to soak the earth like rain and snow so that it gives bread to the hungry (Is 55:10f). Something heavenly was sown into the earth, and the one now returning to the Father, being the heavenly Head of the still earthly Church, henceforth establishes an indissoluble bond between earth and heaven.

He expresses his return home to the Father symbolically, through his elevation from the surface of the earth and by the cloud that conceals him. Once again what is involved here is not change of location within the world but a transformation of state. In the Old Testament, too, the cloud is a symbol for God's presence even in his concealment. It was this same cloud which, at once in radiance and concealment, had enwrapped the transfigured Lord on Mount Tabor. His present concealment within the cloud shows that he is disappearing into the glory of God and that, by the same token, he is drawing up along with himself the yearning of both the Church and the whole world.

For the homeland for which mankind yearns is God. It is not man that is at home in the world, but rather the world in man. It is for man's sake that the world is there; the world is man's substructure, that which makes all his wandering possible; when man reaches his goal then the world reaches its own goal with him. But, again, we are not speaking of a spatial change—as if man had to go out of the world to pass over to God. Rather, it is their state that man and the world which belongs to him must change: they are transferred to a state of being which is conformed to the Son who has returned home, a state which quenches man's yearning and brings the sighing of all creatures to an end, the state in which God is all in all. This had been the Creator's intention from the beginning: that the creature should feel totally at home within itself only when it is in God; that man should be wholly free only when he abides in the eternal Freedom.

For the time being the Head of the Church has been raised up to God so that the Church should exert herself for existing within the huge expanses of her proper habitation in God. For, seen from below, a distance is created which awakens and intensifies our yearning; but this distance is one that is lived in God—spent in believing, hoping and loving—so that it is an intensification of the divine life in those that remain behind.

It is a distance not intended to be overcome in the present time, by pure contemplation, for instance. The angels rebuke the disciples who are looking up to heaven: "You men of Galilee, why do you stand there staring up to heaven?" There is another way to be close to the ascended Lord: "As the Father has sent me, so do I send you." Just as Christ, going forth from the Father to the earth, did the will of the Father and in so doing was with him, so too those who are sent by Christ will be united with him by fulfilling his mandate. And right in the midst of this carrying out of their mission there is the hidden eucharistic presence of the Lord: "I am with you until the end of the world." This is the unseeing of faith, which intensifies the longing for him through the knowledge of his presence. This is the presence of the Beloved in a dark night which intensifies the yearning for the daylight: "until the morning-star rises in your hearts" (2 Pet 1:19). Holy Scripture closes with the yearning cry: "Come, Lord Jesus!" and the answer: "Yes, I am coming soon."

The condition of the Lord's Mother after her Son's Ascension is very mysterious, but it is exemplary for the Church and for each believer. Once more she must let her Son go away. She has done this all through her life, very often with anxiety and sorrow. And now she places him definitively in the hands of the Father. In this there is no longer anything sorrowful, and yet there is a renunciation. For the Son is going into hiddenness, and Mary belongs to the Church so much that she wants to have the same concealed faith as the Church.

This faith is neither mystical vision nor uncertainty; rather, it is filled with the certainty of the promise of final fulfillment. It is beyond doubt that Mary, that the holy Church, will come into

118

heaven, and that Mary-the-Church therefore possesses the certainty of salvation. The only open question is whether we, the individual believers, want to live within this living faith and in conformity to it. For Mary-the-Church a faith which is certain of salvation is a fulfillment in spite of its darkness, because such faith widens the heart to God's dimensions and because no opposition can be said to exist between longing's flight to God and repose in God.

At an essential level, the darkness of faith is already joy. And, indeed, it is not so much a foretaste of joy at the fact that our present faith will be transformed into vision, as joy in the fact that the Son has fulfilled his mission and has now returned to the arms of the Father—joy that God is happy at the success of his plan of salvation. And this happiness already contains the happiness of the world, whether it feels it at present or not. "If you loved me you would rejoice that I go to the Father" (Jn 14:28). The believer rejoices with God and in God. In this way he learns true joy, which looks away from itself and rejoices with the Beloved and for him. Only with this joy will we in the end be able to enter into God's eternal bliss. And it is precisely with this joy existing between Father and Son that the Holy Spirit fills us. This is the Spirit for which the Church, gathered around Mary, waits intently after the Ascension.

## 3

*And blessed is the fruit of your womb*

## JESUS

*who sent us the Holy Spirit*

T HE SPIRIT whom the Son sends to us from the Father on Pentecost is the Spirit of the eternal dialogue of love between Father and Son. He is the speech of God become a person. We are introduced into this language; until now it had been for us a mysterious foreign language, but when the tongues of fire came down upon the Church it became our real "mother tongue". The first word which we, as children of God, learn to stammer in it is the word "Abba!", which is taught to us by God's Spirit, as Paul says expressly two times (Rom 8:15; Gal 4:6). With this childlike word we address not men but God, in the language which is his own and which he understands.

The Holy Spirit given to us is, thus, in the very first place, a Spirit of dialogue with God—a Spirit of prayer—and only on this basis is he a Spirit of dialogue with man—a Spirit of mission.

The prayer which the Son taught us and which begins with the word "Abba, Father!" is essentially a prayer in the language of God: each of the desires expressed in it corresponds to a desire on the part of God. The Hail Mary too is a prayer of the Spirit, for the Angel naturally greeted Mary in the Holy Spirit when he promised her that the Spirit would overshadow her. And it is expressly said that when Elizabeth encountered Mary she was filled with the Holy Spirit and blessed both the Mother and the Child with a *loud* voice full of the Spirit. Thus it is a prayer consisting of inspired words. We too, therefore, should desire that all our prayers be inspired by the Spirit. For prayers are words in the language of God, which is spoken and understood in heaven. There a purely earthly and egotistic language could be neither spoken nor understood. In order to be inspired we need not reflect on the Holy Spirit at every prayer; but each of our prayers should be made in the Spirit who is a Spirit between Father and Son, between the Son become man, whom we know, and the invisible Father, to whom the Son has always referred us. There is room within this space for the whole world with all its concerns; but in order to be transformed into authentic prayer, worldly concerns must expressly be transferred into this space. It is not difficult to imagine whether a petition which I present to the Father is conceivable on the lips of the Son. If it is, then this petition will never have a merely private but always an ecclesial character. That prayer would not revolve around an isolated subject, but around one who, as a member of the Church who lives in and for an ecclesial mission, is praying for the necessary grace to fulfill it: for purity and courage, for clarity and trust, for understanding and selflessness—for everything needed by a person who, through his life and example, would like to be an apostle of Christ.

Thus the spirit of prayer of itself becomes a spirit of mission. After being gathered for forty days with Mary in dialogue with God, the Church receives the gift of tongues on Pentecost so that she can make herself understood to all peoples. She does not first need to reflect for long on how she can translate Christ's message into the conceptual language of a foreign culture and of a new time; this is infused into the Church with genuine prayer. Nor does she have to construct fancy speeches with which to defend herself before the tribunal of the wise of this world and of the authorities, "for what you are to say will be given to you in that hour; for it is not you who speak, but the Spirit of your Father speaking through you" (Mt 10:19f). In the apostolate, therefore, what is imperative is not at all to learn certain catechism truths by heart and then to recite them back at people, nor to devise all on one's own a language which one thinks *must* be understood by the other. The essential thing, rather, is to live, to think and to speak from the wellspring of the triune life. To be sure, understanding does belong to the gifts of the Holy Spirit, but this is an understanding in God which, as with Christ or Paul, can often enough appear to be human foolishness. Neither the Lord nor his apostle veils or thins down the divine truth the better to communicate it. There is a human defenselessness which appeals to the unarmored heart of one's fellow man and gains admittance to it if this heart is willing.

With this we have already made a third point: namely, that the spirit of prayer and of mission is always an ecclesial and, therefore, a Marian spirit. For if Mary originally received the Spirit of the Incarnation with her whole spiritual-corporeal being—which made her become the archetype of the Church—then the Church now receives this Spirit as a totality, and every member of the Church receives the ecclesial Spirit according to his participation in the prayer and the mission of the Church. No believer ever receives the Spirit in a private sense, but always from the totality and for the totality of the Church. Only the Church is the Bride; the individual believer partakes of her reality as bride in the measure in which his soul widens to utter Mary's word of assent, which knows no bounds. But if the Spirit is not private, yet it is personal, as is proven by his activity in the Marian "Cycle of the Beginning". And he works all the more personally the more anonymously the individual puts himself at the disposal of God's plan for the salvation of mankind.

The saints have always lived this paradox before our very eyes: they forget themselves in their prayer and in the fulfillment of their mission, and because of this the Spirit can chisel in them the unique and incomparable features which are their own. Mary only wants to be the maiden who is available for everything her Lord calls her to do, but precisely this "for everything" raises her in all her uniqueness above the rest of men. As the perfect vessel of the Spirit she is blessed among all women, and if he so will, the Spirit can even form her to be the Queen of All the Saints. Her whole attitude is not changed by this; she remains what she always was. "My spirit rejoices in God my Savior, for he has regarded the low estate of his handmaiden. For behold, henceforth all generations will call me blessed."

## 4

*And blessed is the fruit of your womb*

## JESUS

*who took you, O Virgin, up into heaven*

THOSE WHO HAVE WHOLLY PUT THEMSELVES in the hands of God are also wholly accepted by God and wholly perfected by him. Mary's total submission was such that, along with her whole soul, she also offered up her whole body, and this is precisely what God needed in order to realize his plan of salvation. It is just this which is termed Mary's "anticipated redemption": that already in eternity (when the Son offered himself to the Father, when the Father accepted his offer and sent him, and when the Spirit was ready to mediate between heaven and earth) God included Mary's word of assent as an indispensable part of his plan. In order for the Son to be able to take on a genuinely human body, he had for a time to be, inseparably, "one flesh" with his Mother; but the assumption of *this* flesh from the Mother's body required nothing less than *this* word of assent. In a certain sense, within God's plan Mary's word of assent pre-exists even her; to be sure, she will utter it on earth and realize it through her life; but her word of assent will draw her back up into heaven in her totality.

All her being and actions, naturally, are but a service to her Son. He stands in the center. But he cannot be an isolated man without his fellow man, without a woman companion. An "isolated man" is a contradiction in terms. And here we must pay close attention to the particular manner in which he is human: he is the one *in* whom all others are to find their salvation. His body had room enough to take on itself the sin of all; he also cleared sufficient room in himself in order to harbor within himself —in the mystery of the Eucharist—the reality of all others: the Church, as Christ's Body, is "produced" by participation in the one Bread (1 Cor 10:17). Jesus' body is everything but a private body; like his soul and his spirit, his body is one which is distributed, which is lavished on the whole world. And it is in heaven that he best does this, because it is in heaven and from heaven that he not only sends his and the Father's Spirit, but also distributes his Body through all ages of ages. But this reality, whereby the Church becomes one flesh with him through the Eucharist, has its irreversible origin in the fact that, from the outset, he has always been one flesh with Mary. And in heaven the beginning and the end are but one.

To be sure, by virtue of her Son's work Mary is transformed into the Church, whom he creates from himself as his immaculate Bride (Eph 5:27); she does not, however, disappear as the individual person she is, but rather, at the same time as she becomes the Church, she also goes into the Church as one of her members. She is the part and she is the whole, which is fashioned after her model and oriented toward her holiness. She is the individual woman who is also the protective mantle under which Christians gather to form the Church. She is an individual saint in heaven, and at the same time she is the heavenly Jerusalem, "adorned as the Bride of the Lamb" (Rev 21:2), who has been there from the outset so that those who come to heaven can enter in. Just as Mary was redeemed in advance so that the Word could become Flesh, so too—now that heaven is accessible to man through Christ's death and resurrection—the holy City, the universal Church, the Communion of Saints is there already in full perfection, so that those who are sanctified can be incorporated into it.

All of this results from an in-depth meditation

on the biblical texts if they are seen alongside each other and if their interior consequences are thought through. It is not of moment that the insight into this perfecting of Mary cannot be traced back to the very earliest Christian centuries: the thorough reflection on revelation and its deeper implications requires a certain span of time. And the hidden truth concerning Mary-the-Church entered very early as an essential aspect of the truth about the Son of the Father and the conditions for his incarnation not only into the consciousness of isolated theologians, but of the Christian people, which has the instinct for the interior balances of the faith.

Surely it cannot be doubted that Mary really died a human death; she did not simply pass from an earthly into a heavenly state. Even if death, as we know it today, "came into the world through sin", nevertheless Christ took precisely this death of sin upon himself in order to expiate it from within and transform it into an act of free self-surrender to the Father. It could be objected that Mary died spiritually under the Cross along with the Son, and that in this way she made possible the inclusion, within her consent, of the most difficult thing that can be asked of man—his self-surrender: after this sacrifice she has nothing left to sacrifice. We reply that Mary also stands within Eve's physical descent and that therefore, as a member of the human race, she is subject to the law of death. But the difference with Mary is that there can no longer be anything forcibly imposed about her death. While the sinner is compelled at his death to place his spirit back into the hands of his Creator and Father, Mary has long achieved this perfect and willing self-surrender. The fact that her earthly life is taken from her is, in her spirit, only the final form of her letting God do as he will: "Be it done to me according to your word."

This is why it is quite fitting to call upon our Mother precisely at the decisive hour of our crossing: "now and at the hour of our death". Starting with her first word of assent, she daily died for God and into God; she practiced the act of self-surrender so often that she became the Great Expert in Christian living, so to speak. She lived continually in the transition from life in her own self to life in God. And when with our last breath we perhaps breathe our last prayer, she will see our poverty, and repeat the word which she uttered in Cana: "They have no more wine." And to the servants who accompany us on our passage —the angels—she will say: "Do everything he tells you."

If we learn to die from her who learned to die in the manner of her Son, then we need not be worried about what will become of our human totality after our death. It will be God's business that we reach him not as mere halves of ourselves, but as whole persons. With Christ and with Mary the created world has already been taken up into transformation and transfiguration, and the Last Day has already begun. World history does indeed continue still, but in eternal life there is no time that corresponds to historical time. We cannot, of course, plumb the mystery of our bodily resurrection; it is quite enough for us to know that the heavenly City—Christ, Head and Body, Christ, Bridegroom and Bride—will be there corporeally when we make our crossing to take us up into itself. And just as this Christ in heaven is, at the same time, the Christ who distributes himself eucharistically on earth and thus builds up the earthly Church, so even our heavenly joy will in part consist in our working with Christ in the perfecting of our earthly brothers and in our being connecting links between earth and heaven.

## 5

*And blessed is the fruit of your womb*

## JESUS

*who crowned you, O Virgin, in heaven*

I N THIS LAST MYSTERY we look less at the Crowned
than at the hand of the Crowner—the triune
God himself. He himself is the crown that de-
scends upon all that she is. He crowns the three
crowns of these mysteries: those of the beginning, those of the transition and those of the
consummation.

These have all been mysteries of mutual understanding, of mutual agreement, mysteries which
partly took place in full public view, like the
scenes of the Passion, and partly in concealment,
like most of the scenes in the life of Mary. At first
the veil is lifted up a little: Elizabeth and Simeon
have a presentiment of what it conceals; but then
the veil falls ever more deeply over the life of
Mary. The Son's accompaniment by his Mother is

totally unobtrusive, and this relationship is veiled even more deeply by the Son's rejections of her. Only one Evangelist mentions her standing at the foot of the cross and her bond with the Beloved Disciple, and only one reports, almost incidentally, the fact that she was present at the prayer of the Church. Then she disappears altogether. "Blessed is the womb that bore you and the breasts that nursed you," cries from among the people the woman who suspected something of the hidden mystery: from the person of the Son she recognizes the nature of the Mother. But even here the Son draws the veil by universalizing his Mother's case and applying this praise to all anonymous persons in the Church who imitate his Mother: "Yes, they are surely blessed who hear God's Word and keep it."

And now light streams down from the crown on this long, hidden, seemingly insignificant and even useless daily existence that was Mary's. It lights up all the lowest and smallest tasks of a household: washing, cooking, sewing, sweeping the house (like the woman in the parable, whom he certainly modeled after his Mother), looking after the men's needs, dealing with neighbors who were not perhaps always friendly. . . . The most usual thing in the lives of the saints is the gray of day-to-day existence.

But what is wholly overlooked by the world can be brought out by God as being most precious, worthy to be placed on the bushel basket. "He has cast down the mighty from their throne," sings Mary, "and has raised up the lowly." Yes, those lowly ones who are perhaps much more unregarded than Mary, about whom in the end we know many things. We know more about her than about any other woman in Sacred Scripture. But what is revealed about her is shown to us for the Son's sake, in order to make plain in the Mother the nature of the Son and also the way of following after him. Whenever any light falls on her, she appears as the Maiden, the Helpmate. She is this even as the Queen, for whoever is crowned receives both the royal dignity and the royal burden. She is raised up precisely as the lowly one. She is called Queen of the Angels because, together with her Son, she descended lower than the angels to serve mankind and to suffer for it. She is called Queen of the Apostles because she committed herself to the work of her Son—the Church—more deeply, earlier and more thoroughly than they. Being men, the Apostles and their successors only hold an office in the Church; but Mary, being a woman, represents the whole Church to her Lord and Bridegroom. She is the Queen of All the Saints because her "little

way"—her way of simple but radical faith—
becomes the standard by which to measure all
other ways of sanctity, all exalted and all lowly
ways, the ways of all mystics and martyrs, of all
charismatics and missionaries, of all Christians in
all orders and in all the world.

A queen enjoys full power, even with regard to
the king. Mary's fullness of power is expressed
in her intercession for us and her mediation of
graces, so that we receive all personal graces from
God and Christ always as members of the holy
Church—and, therefore, as children of Mary.
But it is the King himself who is the almighty
intercessor for sinners before the Father (Heb 8:6f;
1 Jn 2:1), so that Christ and his Body, the holy
Church, constitute one single principle of mediation. For this reason we ought not to conceive of
the Judgment as if Christ were only the Judge and
Mary the intercessor, perhaps along with some
other saints. Something of this image may be
retained insofar as the Son has really received all
judgment from the Father (Jn 5:27); he has himself
often expressed his consciousness of possessing
this fullness of power. But he will never divide his
function as Judge from his function as Redeemer;
this is why Mary and the interceding Church will
never take a position against him but will always
stand on his side. Because he has bestowed on us

his Holy Spirit and given us his Body, Christ is the wellspring of the Communion of Saints, which is nothing other than the full power of every loving person to communicate to others in need his own store of divine gifts. And this is the essence of the whole work of redemption, which the Father has permitted and made possible through his goodness.

But it is in Mary that we can best grasp what the Communion of Saints is for us men. For if each of God's gifts also contains his petition and demand that we should receive the gift and reciprocate it, it is in Mary that the correspondence between gift and self-giving, reception and thanksgiving attains perfection. This makes man capable of being fruitful along with the eternal fruitfulness of God, so that out of his completed self-surrender he can, in turn, form a gift and thus transmit the divine grace further through himself. Mary-the-Church keeps no grace for herself; she receives grace in order to transmit it. This is what a mother does. We are the children of Mary's fruitfulness, and her fruitfulness has been given her that she might receive and fulfill the fruitfulness of her Spouse. And this obliges us, too, ourselves to be the Church and to become inserted into this cycle of reception and transmission.

Surely this circulation of life and love will not

come to a halt in heaven; rather, it is there that it will reach genuine efficacy. If heaven is being in God, and if the triune God is an endless exchange among the persons of God the Father, God the Son and God the Holy Spirit, then God will draw his perfected creation into this flow of divine life. At that time, as the Lord of the Apocalypse says, each one shall receive a new name "which no one knows" except God and himself. Each one will finally know who he is in reality, and consequently each will at this time be able to make of himself a fully authentic and unique gift. And this self-giving will be common to all, so that we will not only plunge eternally into God's ever newer depths, but also into the inexhaustible depths of our fellow creatures, both angels and men. It will not be, however, as if everything will suddenly lie exposed before us, as if we were now to peer into everything with a sort of rude indiscretion and nothing more remained to be discovered. This is not possible because God is infinite freedom and every created person participates in this freedom, which must manifest itself of its own accord in order to be known. For this reason heaven will be the opposite of boredom. For all eternity God will remain a mystery, and we will not ever exhaust the full depth of the grace whereby each of us is permitted to participate in this mystery by the very fact that we *are* and that we can love one another.

And if at times the prayer of Mary on earth appears to us to be monotonous because the same greeting, the same blessing and the same petition always succeed one another, we should also remember that this prayer, when uttered in eternal life, is an expression of the blessed cycle whereby God is always greeting us anew as his children and we are endlessly sending up to him a grateful sacrifice of praise.

## Scriptural Epilogue

*A great portent appeared in heaven, a woman clothed with the sun, with the moon under her feet, and on her head a crown of twelve stars; she was with child and she cried out in her pangs of birth, in anguish for delivery. And another portent appeared in heaven; behold, a great red dragon, with seven heads and ten horns, and seven diadems upon his heads. His tail swept down a third of the stars of heaven, and cast them to the earth. And the dragon stood before the woman who was about to bear a child, that he might devour her child when she brought it forth; she brought forth a male child, one who is to rule all the nations with a rod of iron, but her child was caught up to God and to his throne, and the woman fled into the wilderness, where she has a place prepared*

The Scriptural Epilogue is taken from Revelation 12, Revised Standard Version of the Bible, © 1973.

*by God, in which to be nourished for one thousand two hundred and sixty days.*

*Now war arose in heaven, Michael and his angels fighting against the dragon; and the dragon and his angels fought, but they were defeated and there was no longer any place for them in heaven. And the great dragon was thrown down, that ancient serpent, who is called the Devil and Satan, the deceiver of the whole world—he was thrown down to the earth, and his angels were thrown down with him. And I heard a loud voice in heaven, saying, "Now the salvation and the power and the kingdom of our God and the authority of his Christ have come, for the accuser of our brethren has been thrown down, who accuses them day and night before our God. And they have conquered him by the blood of the Lamb and by the word of their testimony, for they loved not their lives even unto death. Rejoice then, O heaven and you that dwell therein! But woe to you, O earth and sea, for the devil has come down to you in great wrath, because he knows that his time is short."*

*And when the dragon saw that he had been thrown down to the earth, he pursued the woman who had borne the male child. But the woman was given two wings of the great eagle that she might fly from the serpent into the wilderness, to the place where she is to be nourished for a time, and times, and half a time. The serpent poured water like a river out of his mouth after the woman, to sweep her away with the flood. But the earth came to the help of the woman, and the earth opened its mouth and swallowed the river which the dragon had poured from his mouth. Then the dragon was angry with the woman, and went off to make war on the rest of her offspring, on those who keep the commandments of God and bear testimony to Jesus. And he stood on the sand of the sea.*

Apocalypse 12

# CONCLUDING NOTE

The purpose of these short meditations has by now become clear to the reader. Our aim has been to free the prayer of the Rosary from a certain narrowness, alien to Mary's own spirit and easily leading to monotony, and to nourish it, in a manner corresponding to her spirit, with the fullness of God's saving thoughts and saving deeds for the world. Mary's essence and efficacy in this prayer are founded on her mediation: between God and the world, between Christ and the Church, between spirit and flesh, between the two states of life in the Church, between the world of the saints and that of sinners. Mary stands at all crossroads pointing the way. But prayer to the Mediatrix has meaning only if what she is to mediate remains within the field of vision of the person praying:

and this is the world's salvation through Christ, the Son of God, our Lord, whom the Father gives to us and who, together with the Father, pours down the Holy Spirit into our hearts.

LAUS DEO VIRGINIQUE MATRI